February 11, 1955

Mark - Joinell

the world ... now in

2005

?

HE'S 50!

over the
hill he goes

Ha Ha Ha

stay young and
have fun

Love
Katia + Jesse +
Skyp

WHAT A YEAR IT WAS!

1955

A walk back in time to revisit
what life was like in the year that
has special meaning for you...

Congratulations
and
Best Wishes

To

From

DEDICATION

To the Girls of 32nd Street
Carol, Cookie, Sarah, Kathy, Rozzie and Loretta
and
My Late Brother, Jerry Gsell, Who Survived the '50s With Me

Series Created By • Beverly Cohn
Designers • Peter Hess & Marguerite Jones
Research • Laurie Cohn Rosenthal

Special thanks to Kenny Bookbinder for his invaluable help with the Sports section.

CONTENTS

PRESIDENT EISENHOWER STRICKEN!

CIRCULATION

DAILY

A stunned nation learns that its president has suffered a heart attack while vacationing at the Denver home of his mother-in-law, Mrs. John Doud.

Major **John Eisenhower** *(left)* and press secretary **James Haggerty** rush to the president's bedside, from which physicians issue cautiously optimistic bulletins.

As an anxious nation awaits, newsmen converge on the press secretary in an improvised pressroom.

Vice President **Nixon** leaves for emergency meetings.

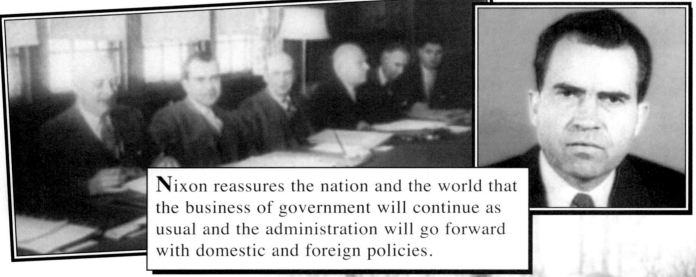

Nixon reassures the nation and the world that the business of government will continue as usual and the administration will go forward with domestic and foreign policies.

By year's end, Ike recovers sufficiently to hold cabinet meetings in his mountain retreat.

WHAT A YEAR IT WAS!

Eisenhower's Open Sky

Heads of the Soviet Union, England, France and the United States gather in Geneva for the first Big Four summit held since the end of World War II in an attempt to capture the "Geneva Spirit."

Above, left to right:
Premier Nikolay Bulganin (U.S.S.R.),
President Dwight D. Eisenhower (U.S.A.),
Premier Edgar Faure (France) and
Prime Minister, Sir Anthony Eden (Britain)

Soviet Premier Nikolay Bulganin (left)
and President Dwight D. Eisenhower

President Eisenhower surprises the world leaders with his dramatic proposal of the "Open Sky" inspection of military installations as a barrier to unexpected attacks. It is a plea for an insured peace.

Subsequent meetings of the Big Four foreign ministers fail to produce a definitive peace agreement.

MOST COMFORTABLE WAY
TO GET THERE FAST

QUIET LUXURY TO MAKE THE TIME FLY - NEW SPEED TO SHORTEN THE DISTANCE

Largest, Roomiest
Airliner in the World

*Far Quieter for
Greater Comfort*

Wider Aisles & Seats

Larger Windows

Finest Air Conditioning

Restful 5-Cabin Privacy

Congenial
Starlight Lounge

Henry Dreyfuss Interiors

The Fastest
Constellation Ever Built

For all the speed, and quiet comfort, too, fly Super Constellations over every ocean and continent on these 20 leading airlines: AIR FRANCE • AIR-INDIA INTERNATIONAL
AVIANCA • CUBANA • DEUTSCHE LUFTHANSA
EASTERN AIR LINES • FLYING TIGER LINE • IBERIA
KLM • LAV • NORTHWEST ORIENT AIRLINES
PAKISTAN INTERNATIONAL • QANTAS
SEABOARD 7 WESTERN • SLICK AIRWAYS • TAP
THAI AIRWAYS • TRANS-CANADA AIR LINES
TWA-TRANS WORLD AIRLINES • VARIG

LOCKHEED SUPER CONSTELLATION

Look to Lockheed for Leadership

The UNITED NATIONS celebrates its 10th anniversary and reaffirms the right of all nations to determine their own status.

1955

16 new members

12 free nations and 4 from the Communist bloc are admitted to the United Nations after a 5-year deadlock. The world body now numbers 76.

ALBANIA
AUSTRIA
BULGARIA
CAMBODIA
CEYLON
FINLAND
HUNGARY
IRELAND
ITALY
JORDAN
LAOS
LIBYA
NEPAL
PORTUGAL
ROMANIA
SPAIN

1955

Sam Rayburn is elected Speaker of the House of Representatives.

Democrat **Adlai Stevenson** declares his presidential candidacy.

✶ ✶ ✶

W. Averell Harriman is sworn in as governor of New York.

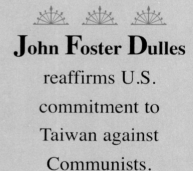

John Foster Dulles reaffirms U.S. commitment to Taiwan against Communists.

✭ U.S. Senate votes to continue its investigation of Communism.

✭ House of Representatives votes itself a 50% pay hike.

✭ Following ratification of the SEATO treaty by U.S. Congress, eight nations meet in Bangkok for first SEATO council.

✭ President Eisenhower says U.S. will use A-bomb in the event of war.

W. Averell Harriman (left) and Adlai Stevenson

WHAT A YEAR IT WAS!

NIKOLAY BULGANIN replaces GEORGY MALENKOV as premier of the Soviet Union.

Nikolay Bulganin

SOVIET UNION

- Soviet Communist Party Secretary Nikita Khrushchev reopens relations with Yugoslav President Tito.
- Khrushchev arrives in Belgrade where he and Tito shake hands, ending the seven-year feud between their countries.
- Khrushchev delivers a speech in India condemning British colonialism.
- Indian Prime Minister Nehru and Soviet Premier Bulganin reaffirm their friendship.
- Canada and the U.S.S.R. grant each other most-favored-nation status.

U.S. Post Office Refuses To Deliver Soviet Newspapers, *PRAVDA* And *IZVESTIA*, To American Subscribers.

ПРАВДА

NYET!

Soviets pledge to shut down bases on foreign soil.

The U.S. bars the photography or sketching of U.S. military installations by Soviet citizens living in the U.S.

Soviets shoot down U.S. naval patrol plane over the Bering Strait and offer to pay for part of the damage.

The Soviet Union and Czechoslovakia officially end their state of war status with Germany.

Yugoslavia's Marshal Tito (left, in white jacket) and Nikita Khrushchev (right)

EUROPE

Sir **Winston Churchill** resigns as prime minister of the United Kingdom— **Sir Anthony Eden** is named as successor.

Winston Churchill

Clement Attlee, head of the British Labour Party for 20 years, retires and is succeeded by **Hugh Gaitskell**.

Britain turns to the International Court of Justice to seek recognition of its sovereignty over the Falkland Islands.

Britain announces home rule plan for Cyprus.

Edgar Faure succeeds Pierre Mendès-France as prime minister following the French National Assembly's rejection of Mendès-France's government and cabinet.

Thousands of middle-class French people turn out to hear reactionary **Pierre Poujade** vent his bigotry, including his attack on former prime minister Mendès-France, who Poujade says is not French enough because he drinks milk.

Portugal breaks relations with India after invasion of Goa by Indian nationalists.

Spain's **General Franco** hints **Prince Juan Carlos** will be next head of state.

General Franco and U.S. Secretary of State **John Foster Dulles** affirm close ties.

General Franco

With Socialist and Communist support, Christian Democrat **Giovanni Gronchi** is elected president of Italy.

Andras Hegedus is elected premier of Hungary, succeeding **Imre Nagy**, father of the discredited "new course."

ANTI-GREEK RIOTS SPREAD IN ISTANBUL AND SMYRNA.

The Warsaw Pact, unifying the Eastern bloc nations, creates a formal alliance against NATO.

WHAT A YEAR IT WAS!

The new West German army is officially launched as 101 men receive their certificates.

West German Chancellor **Konrad Adenauer** is invited to Moscow to establish diplomatic and trade ties.

U.S. begins funding of West German rearmament.

After 10 years of Allied occupation, the Federal Republic of Germany becomes a sovereign nation and enters NATO.

17 West German trucks en route to Berlin are seized by East German troops.

40,000 Berliners
gather to denounce the rise of neo-Nazism.

Austria Regains Sovereignty

U.S. Secretary of State **John Foster Dulles**, Soviet Foreign Minister **Vyacheslav Molotov** and British Foreign Minister **Harold Macmillan** sign treaty with Austria ending their 10-year occupation.

From left: Dulles, Molotov and Macmillan

The treaty, signed and sealed

Above: the signing ceremony; the treaty is displayed, below.

*F*reedom comes to Austria after 26 years of foreign rule followed by postwar occupation.

Tearful reunions take place as families are reunited and the Soviet Union returns prisoners.

Freedom-loving people all over the
world are hopeful that someday
the Cold War might end.

Juan Perón addresses his nation in the wake of the civilian-supported military uprising.

Juan Perón surrenders the reins of power to the military and is ousted after a 9-year dictatorship in Argentina.

Perón's pleas for support fall on deaf ears as his long history of persecution of the clergy and his excommunication by the Pope bring the inevitable retribution.

Elements of the army, navy and air force defect to support his ouster.

Crowds in Buenos Aires' Plaza de Mayo

Last to fall is the headquarters of the Labor Confederation, his staunchest supporter.

The destruction is complete and Perón flees to Paraguay.

In the early days of his rule, Perón made himself popular with the masses by forming Latin America's first labor movement, nationalizing foreign industries and making Argentina part of the Third World bloc.

PANAMA signs accord with the U.S. establishing cooperation over canal issues.

Passings

Cordell Hull, 83
Secretary of state under President Franklin D. Roosevelt, Hull helped to organize the United Nations, and was awarded the Nobel Peace Prize in 1945.

Hull

Marshal Alexander Papagos, 71
Greek premier since 1952.

Papagos

King Sri Sri Sri Sri Sri Tribhubana Bir Bikram Jung Bahadur Shah Bahadur Shum Shere Jung Deva, 48
King of Nepal, who, while in India for several months, put his three-year-old grandson on the throne.

1955

Middle East

Egypt to receive arms from the Soviets.

U.S. offers weapons to Egypt to offset Soviet aid.

Egypt pulls out of talks with Israel on Gaza border conflicts.

Egypt, Syria and Jordan agree to unify military commands.

Israeli and Egyptian forces engage in battle in the Gaza area as the U.N. Security Council urges avoidance of violence.

In retaliation for the hanging in Egypt of two Jews as spies, Israeli forces attack Egyptian military posts near the Gaza railway station, killing 36 soldiers and 6 civilians.

Israel and Jordan set up a security zone in the Jerusalem area.

Israel accepts cease-fire along Gaza frontier.

David Ben-Gurion returns to Israeli cabinet as defense minister and is later confirmed as premier of Israel.

Bulgaria shoots down Israeli passenger aircraft.

U.S. Secretary of State Dulles proposes steps to end hostilities between Israel and the Arab world.

TURKEY
MEDITERRANEAN SEA
SYRIA
LEBANON
ISRAEL
IRAQ
IRAN
JORDAN
Nile River
EGYPT
SAUDI ARABIA
PERSIAN GULF
RED SEA
SUDAN

WHAT A YEAR IT WAS!

Your love is just around the corner when you fly by DC-7

Whatever your reason for getting there sooner...

Take the fast one...the DC-7

With its top speed a remarkable 410 miles an hour, the DC-7 wings you with velvet swiftness across the oceans, across the continents — anywhere in the world!

There's unbeatable luxury and comfort, too. The spacious DC-7 cabin is pressurized, air conditioned, sound-proofed and tastefully appointed to make your travel completely restful.

Next trip, get there *sooner*, more *comfortably* — by DC-7. See why *more* people and *more* airlines fly Douglas than all other airplanes *combined!*

DOUGLAS
BUILDERS OF THE DC-8 JETLINER

AFRICA

A South African sign enforcing apartheid

FOR USE BY WHITE PERSONS

THESE PUBLIC PREMISES AND THE AMENITIES THEREOF HAVE BEEN RESERVED FOR THE EXCLUSIVE USE OF WHITE PERSONS.

By Order   Provincial Secretary

VIR GEBRUIK DEUR BLANKES

South African delegate to the United Nations walks out of U.N. debate over apartheid policies.

The ruling Nationalist Party is given additional powers by the South African Parliament.

France declares state of emergency in Algeria.

100 arrested in Algiers, including the secretary general of the Communist Party, in an attempt to get rid of leftist factions.

Following nine months of negotiations, France formalizes the autonomy of Tunisia, accepting home rule for the North African nation.

Algiers

British troops launch attack on Mau-Mau rebels in the mountains of Kenya.

●

Belgium to sell Congolese uranium to Great Britain and the U.S.

WHAT A YEAR IT WAS!

MOROCCO

Martial law is declared in Casablanca, Morocco following fighting between the French and native Moroccans.

Moroccan rebels kill 49 French on anniversary of Sultan ben Youssef's deposition.

North Africa Suffers Serious Death Toll In Fighting Between The French And Algerian And Moroccan Nationalist Groups Intent On Forcing France Out Of North Africa.

Under pressure from France, Moroccan Sultan ben Afra resigns his throne and is replaced by exiled Sultan ben Youssef in a move that France hopes will be viewed as a form of rapprochement rather than appeasement.

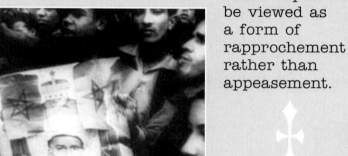

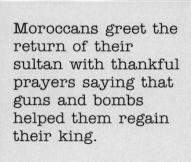

Moroccans greet the return of their sultan with thankful prayers saying that guns and bombs helped them regain their king.

WHO'S WHO ON THE HIGHWAY

This page will help you to identify the license plates for all 48 States and the Canadian Provinces. It will also remind you that wherever you drive, one of the 38,000 Atlas dealers in the U.S. and Canada is nearby — ready with dependable Atlas products and service. He'll honor the famous Guarantees on Atlas tires and batteries. Remember, too: Atlas dealers are specifically trained to give top quality service on all types of tubeless tires.

ATLAS TIRES
BATTERIES
ACCESSORIES

DRIVE WITH CARE . . . OBEY TRAFFIC SIGNS!

ASIA

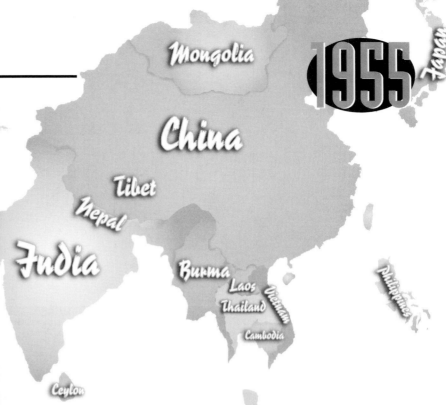

Mongolia

1955

Japan

China

Tibet

Nepal

India

Burma

Laos

Thailand

Vietnam

Cambodia

Philippines

Ceylon

General Maxwell D. Taylor is appointed U.S. commander in chief in the Far East and head of the U.N. Far East Command.

- 100 Communist China planes raid Nationalists on Tachen Islands.
- U.S. Congress passes bill allowing mobilization if China attacks Taiwan.
- Military service becomes mandatory in China.
- Chinese Nationalists evacuate Nanchi Island following Communist invasion.
- Communist China releases four U.S. airmen accused of espionage.
- U.S. establishes air bases in Taiwan.
- 11 U.S. fliers are freed in Peking as talks with U.S. begin.
- Peking agrees to free all remaining U.S. civilians in Communist China.

Crown Prince Mahendra Bir Bikram Shah Dev named king of Nepal.

Nepal and Communist China establish diplomatic relations.

Ichiro Hatoyama reelected premier of Japan.

VIETNAM

- French ship *Esperance* leaves Haiphong in North Vietnam, ending evacuation of troops.
- France signs first trade agreement with Hanoi.
- Rival factions wage civil war in the streets of Saigon, with Premier **Ngo Dinh Diem** emerging victorious following a takeover attempt by General **Nguyen Van Vy**.
- Premier Ngo Dinh Diem declares South Vietnam a republic and becomes its first president.
- Premier Ngo Dinh Diem declares that his country is not tied by Geneva Accord.
- U.S. approves $100,000,000 for economic and technical aid to Cambodia, Laos and South Vietnam.

Ngo Dinh Diem

WHAT A YEAR IT WAS!

argus A-4: This low-priced, big-value 35mm camera takes magnificent color slides. Its Cintar f:3.5 lens is the fastest of any American-made 35mm camera in its price class. It has precision shutter, Color-matic settings, built-in flash synchronization.

Only **$32.50** *Case: $3.65 Flash: $3.80*

argus 75 camera kit: The Argus 75 is the world's easiest camera to use. It has a big, picture-size viewfinder, a lens that's always in focus, and a double-exposure preventer. Kit includes camera, plug-in flashgun and shield, flash bulbs, batteries and film—everything for wonderful pictures! *Only* **$19.95** *complete.*

argus super 75 color kit: The Super 75's full-focusing, three-stop, f:8 lens shoots color indoors or out, night or day, close-up too. Kit includes flashgun, flash guard, leather carrying case, color flash bulbs, batteries, color film.

Only **$32.75** *complete.*

argus has
a gift for making people happy!

Big people, small people . . . men people, women people . . . young people, old people . . . they all become *happy people* when the Christmas wrappings open up on an Argus!

An Argus camera, for example, will let them take wonderful pictures on beaches or in caves . . . in houses where Washington slept or in hotels where they slept . . . anywhere the mood strikes them. And an Argus projector will let them see their color slides as big as life—and just as true.

So put happiness on your Christmas shopping list right now. You can pick it up at your Argus dealer's the next time you pass his way.

argus

Manufacturers of precision photographic and optical instruments

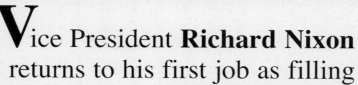

Vice President **Richard Nixon** returns to his first job as filling station attendant to help launch the MARCH OF DIMES campaign.

He has lost none of the skills he picked up in his college years while working summers in his father's gas station.

Frank Sinatra and Ava Gardner

FRANK SINATRA is mobbed at the airport on his first visit to Australia.

WOULD SHE RATHER ACT WITH A COATRACK?

En route to Dublin for a vacation, screen star **Ava Gardner** dodges questions about appearing in *St. Louis Woman* with her estranged husband, **Frank Sinatra**.

NOW, GIRLS—PUT AWAY THOSE CLAWS

Lady Astor and **Tallulah Bankhead** trade nasty barbs as Astor refuses to appear at an event together, saying she is "repelled by her," to which Bankhead replies, "Say that I called her a bitch, dahling."

CAN "DECISIONS FOR MOSES" BE FAR OFF?

American evangelist **BILLY GRAHAM** arrives in Paris for a five-day crusade where he preaches to 42,000 people, convincing 2,254 to make "decisions for Christ."

• • •

As Madison Square Garden vendors hawk coffee, soda pop and frankfurters, Rev. Billy Graham takes on the devil before a capacity crowd.

Sam Rayburn, Speaker of the House, and **Joe Martin**, House Minority Leader, pay a backstage call on **Tallulah Bankhead** following her performance in *Dear Charles* in Washington, D.C.

Gina Lollobrigida hailed as reigning queen of the Italian film industry.

U.S. jazzman **LIONEL HAMPTON** *dazzles an Israeli audience with his jazzed-up version of the Hora, a popular folk dance.*

Kirk Douglas sings with **Marlene Dietrich** and **Gina Lollobrigida** at a polio benefit held at Monte Carlo's Summer Sporting Club.

Tallulah Bankhead

Writing a guest column in a Hollywood paper, 38-year-old television comedienne **JUNE HAVOC** extols the virtues of older men, saying "there are very few interesting men under 65" and that she always "looks for a shiny head or silver hair and a twinkle in the eye."

Grace Kelly

NOT A BUBBLE IN SIGHT

Grace Kelly reveals the secret of her fresh-scrubbed look—she never uses soap on her face.

WHAT A YEAR IT WAS!

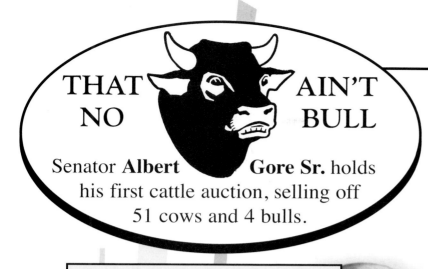

THAT NO AIN'T BULL

Senator **Albert Gore Sr.** holds his first cattle auction, selling off 51 cows and 4 bulls.

Octogenarian **Emily Post** celebrates the 82nd printing of her book ETIQUETTE: THE BLUE BOOK OF SOCIAL USAGE. Important advice: While it is now acceptable practice to dine alone in a gentleman's apartment, to be proper you must leave before 10:00 p.m.

Adlai Stevenson

WHEN WINNY SPEAKS, *TIME* LISTENS

Sir Winston and Lady Churchill dine with U.S. Ambassador to Italy **Clare Boothe Luce** and **Henry R. Luce**, Time Inc.'s editor-in-chief, who announces that Sir Winston's book *A History of the English-Speaking Peoples* will be serialized in *Time.*

THE ELOQUENT ORATOR WILL SPEAK

1952 presidential candidate **Adlai E. Stevenson** will conduct a seminar on law and society at the Northwestern University Law School.

KNOWS HER P'S & Q'S

13-year-old **Sandra Sloss** visits with President **Dwight D. Eisenhower** after winning the National Spelling Bee in Washington by spelling the word "abbacy" correctly.

A REAL HORROR STORY

Broke and a junkie, 72-year-old BELA LUGOSI of *Dracula* fame is admitted to a state hospital for drug addiction.

A VERY PERSONAL "PERSON TO PERSON"

Edward R. Murrow, who has to be in London to cover a story, replaces himself with **Margaret Truman** to interview former president **Harry S. and Mrs. Truman** on Murrow's PERSON TO PERSON television program.

Nelson A. Rockefeller resigns as Ike's special assistant for psychological strategy.

UP IN SMOKE

Interested in the health of his employees, Texas oilman J.S. Bridwell hands out $50 rewards to employees who quit smoking.

WHAT A YEAR IT WAS!

1955

THIS NASTY LADY CAN REALLY BURN YOU UP

Arriving in Washington for a visit, Britain's **Lady Astor** quips, "The only thing I like about rich people is their money."

President Eisenhower is presented with a granddaughter by his son, **Major John Eisenhower**.

BY THE SKIN OF HER MINK

Perle Mesta, encountering rioting Vietnamese students, is badly shaken and says she was lucky to get out of the country with her luggage.

NOW, ABOUT RETURNING THAT ENGAGEMENT RING

Esther Pauline Friedman Lederer, a.k.a. **Ann Landers**, launches her advice column in the *Chicago Sun-Times*.

Pianist Liberace is one of the guests at former world figure skating champion **Sonja Henie's** $15,000 costume party thrown at Ciro's nightclub in Hollywood.

A COLORFUL SPECTACLE

Painter **Pablo Picasso** and his friend playwright **Jean Cocteau** attend the annual bullfight-for-fun fiesta in France where the bull's life is spared.

BEAUTY AND THE NOVELIST

Marilyn Monroe and **Truman Capote** take a spin around the dance floor at Manhattan's posh El Morocco nightclub.

Marilyn Monroe

LET HIM EAT CAKE

Hollywood actress **June Allyson** helps Air Force General **Curtis LeMay** celebrate the ninth anniversary of the formation of the Strategic Air Command by feeding him cake.

74-year-old blind deaf-mute **Helen Keller** arrives in Burma and visits with Premier **U Nu**.

THIS OLD SOLDIER COMMUTES BY LIMOUSINE

Remington Rand's chairman, 75-year-old General **Douglas MacArthur**, whose annual salary is $68,000, commutes from his apartment on the 37th floor of the Waldorf Towers to suburban Connecticut two or three times a week.

A VERY HAPPY NOTE

87-year-old maestro **Arturo Toscanini** arrives from Milan at New York's International Airport where he is met by his son **Walter** and daughter **Wanda**, who is married to pianist **Vladimir Horowitz**.

Toscanini

The toast of Paris, black torch singer **Josephine Baker** charges that U.S. blacks "are treated like dogs" in America's "model democracy."

IT'S ALL RELATIVE— RELATIVELY SPEAKING

After wading through 301 pages of *The Drama of Albert Einstein*, songbird **Dinah Shore** concludes "it's easier to understand relatives than relativity."

A COSMIC EXPERIENCE

As a result of making a $10,000 contribution to the North Side Center Home for Orphans in New York, 26-year-old **Eartha Kitt** has a dream come true when she gets to spend an afternoon at the home of 75-year-old physicist **Albert Einstein**.

WHAT A YEAR IT WAS!

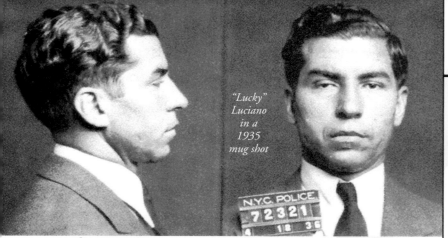

"Lucky" Luciano in a 1935 mug shot

A NECKTIE PARTY WITH A DIFFERENT TWIST

Dining on spaghetti and meatballs in Napoli, Italy, former New York vice czar **Charles "Lucky" Luciano** announces that he is finished with the rackets and will now devote his life to haberdashery, including selling neckties.

FORWARD HIS MAIL C/O SING SING PRISON

Playboy heir to a $3,000,000 margarine fortune, **Minot F. "Mickey" Jelke**, 25, is convicted for the second time of enticing **Pat Ward** and **Marguerite Cordova** to lead lives of prostitution.

U.S. Treasurer **Ivy Baker Priest** is fined $14 for speeding near Brady, Nebraska en route from the capital to her Utah home.

Ivy Baker Priest

ONE MORE LOOP-DE-LOOP AND THAT'S IT!

Setter of the women's unofficial speed record of 708 mph, 37-year-old aviatrix **Jacqueline Auriol** is grounded for a month for reckless piloting.

Jacqueline Auriol

WHAT A YEAR IT WAS!

HOLD THE PICKLES, HOLD THE RELISH, HOLD THE ONIONS

Actor **Robert Mitchum** slaps a $1 million libel suit on *Confidential* magazine, which alleges that Mitchum arrived drunk at a dinner party (which he thought was a masquerade party), took off his clothes, sprinkled himself with ketchup and declared himself a hamburger.

Robert Mitchum

WOE IS THEM

Rita Hayworth and **Dick Haymes** have their hands full. Columbia studios is suing Miss Hayworth for defaulting on a $17,844 note and Dick is facing deportation to his native Argentina by the Justice Department.

INTRIGUE ON LONG ISLAND

Mistaking him for a burglar, **Ann Eden Crowell Woodward** shoots her horse breeder husband, **William Woodward Jr.**, with a rifle.

HIS WRITING IS MUCH BETTER THAN HIS SHOOTING

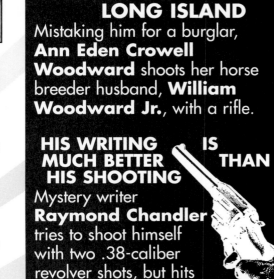

Mystery writer **Raymond Chandler** tries to shoot himself with two .38-caliber revolver shots, but hits the ceiling instead.

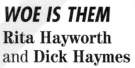

29

1955 — Royal Goings-On

With growing opposition and her fear of unsettling the delicate balance of church, state and throne, **Princess Margaret** chooses duty over love and abandons her plans to marry **Group Captain Peter Townsend**.

THE PRINCE IS STEPPING OUT

Six-year-old **Prince Charles'** homeschooling is about to be augmented as Queen Elizabeth II announces that the bonny young prince will be joining other boys and girls for outings to "museums and other places of interest."

Young Prince Charles

TRAINING DAY FOR THE YOUNG PRINCE

As part of his education, Prince Charles gets a tour of the Trafalgar Square underground station so he can look at London's subway trains.

ROYAL ROMPER ROOM

According to a recent magazine article, Prince Charles, heir to the British throne, is like most six-year-olds—devilish and inquisitive.

WHAT A YEAR IT WAS!

Instead of disappearing at the appointed customary hour, Queen Elizabeth II dances the night away at a party given by American Ambassador to Great Britain **Winthrop Aldrich** held in the huge mansion donated to the U.S. government by five-and-dime heiress **Barbara Hutton** back in 1946. The occasion? An official housewarming to celebrate **George Washington's** birthday.

DON'T STEP IN THE ROYAL HORSE DOO-DOO

Queen Elizabeth II and Princess Margaret stage an impromptu three-furlong horse race at Britain's Ascot Heath track with the princess winning by three lengths.

Queen Elizabeth II bestows the rank and baton of a British Army field marshal upon her uncle, the **Duke of Gloucester**, on the eve of his 55th birthday.

CAN YOU HEAR ME NOW?
The **Duke of Edinburgh** installs a long-range telephone in his sports car so he can keep in touch with his wife, Queen Elizabeth II.

CURTSIES GALORE
500 people, including 13 American debutantes, are presented to Queen Elizabeth II and the Duke of Edinburgh at the rate of one every seven and a half seconds.

HASN'T SHE READ A GOOD BOOK LATELY?
Queen Elizabeth II's annual Honors List, which the press criticizes as "a haven for aging admirals and bureaucrats," includes **Aga Khan**, **Sir Roger Makins** and **John Landy**. Distinctly missing from the 2,000 names are any famous authors or actors.

TALK ABOUT A SATURDAY NIGHT DATE
Princess Margaret shows up at London's Stork Room accompanied by seven male escorts.

Queen Elizabeth II celebrates her birthday by bestowing titles on some of Britain's outstanding nationals, including actor **Alec Guinness**, sculptor **Henry Moore** and **Admiral Earl Mountbatten**.

Queen Elizabeth II

1955

The Royal Family Arrives In Scotland For A Charity Event

The Queen Mother sells an item with a royal "hello" and a friendly word or two.

No matter how insignificant the article may be, it takes on added excitement when sold by royalty.

Both Prince Charles and Princess Anne pitch in. The younger generation's royal salesmanship makes a big hit with their customers.

TRIPPING THE LIFE FANTASTIC

Britain's Princess Margaret sprains her ankle while helping out at a church bazaar in Scotland on the eve of her 25th birthday.

THE OLD KING IS DIGGING THIS

Sweden's **King Gustaf VI Adolph** receives an honorary Doctor of Letters degree at England's Oxford University for his pioneering spade-work as an archaeologist.

King Gustaf VI Adolph

DICKIE DARLING

Admiral of the Fleet, First **Earl Mountbatten of Burma ("Dickie")** arrives at the Admiralty in London and takes office as Britain's First Sea Lord.

The **Duchess of Windsor** is missing from the guest list for a cruise given by her former best friend, 72-year-old party girl **Elsa Maxwell**. Invited guests include Scotland's **Duke and Duchess of Argyll, Prince Aly Khan, Perle Mesta** and **Olivia de Havilland**.

Duchess of Windsor

Handsome **Prince Rainier III** of Monaco examines his newly purchased American car shortly after his arrival in New York. The bachelor prince may find the wife he is seeking in America.

PULLING ROYAL STRINGS

Belgium's **Queen Mother Elisabeth** visits the home of Spanish cellist **Pablo Casals** in the south of France where she accompanies him on her violin as they play a few Beethoven pieces.

HOT TO TROT

Recovered from his heart attack, 77-year-old **Aga Khan** shows up at Paris' Longchamp racetrack with his French-born wife, **the Begum**.

When asked to what he attributes his remarkable success with women, **Prince Aly Khan** laughs and says, "Having money has helped."

SLIP, SLIDING AWAY

82-year-old **King Haakon VII of Norway** breaks his thigh after slipping on a wet bathroom floor and is hospitalized for the first time in his life.

EVEN A SMALL 21-GUN SALUTE

In anticipation of a visit from the **Shah of Iran** and his **Queen Soraya**, the Sans Souci Hotel in Miami Beach runs a red carpet from its lobby to the street, redecorates a 16-room wing as the imperial suite and paints the Shah's coat of arms on every door.

Fireworks fill the sky and there's dancing in the streets as 19-year-old **King Hussein of Jordan** marries his 26-year-old cousin, **Sherifa Dina Abdul Hamid el-Aoun**.

King Hussein

Daddy's home — hours sooner by DC-7

Whatever your reason for getting there faster...

_____*you go fastest by far in a* **DC-7**

You fly up to *50 m.p.h. faster* in the new DC-7 than in any other airliner now in service. With its four giant turbo compound engines, its clean straight lines and single tail, the DC-7 has a top speed of 410 m.p.h.

Unmatched in luxury, too! The Douglas DC-7 has scores of new comforts and conveniences. It is the most restful way to go.

DC *means* **DOUGLAS**

1955

An Air Force Reserve colonel and wartime B-24 wing commander who flew 20 missions, **JAMES STEWART** receives the Air Force's Exceptional Civilian Service award for his help in promoting U.S. air power.

TOPPING IT OFF

Toupee-toting NBC newsman **JOHN CAMERON SWAYZE** is voted the Best-Groomed Newscaster of 1955 by the Barbers of America.

JOHN MARSHALL HARLAN is sworn in to the U.S. Supreme Court.

VICE PRESIDENT RICHARD NIXON makes an impromptu tour of Harlem with an entourage of Global News executives who are going to present Mr. Nixon with a public service award on behalf of the Global News Syndicate.

James Stewart

Capped and gowned, 18-year-old "child star" **MARGARET O'BRIEN** graduates from University High School in West Los Angeles.

DANNY KAYE honored for his work on behalf of UNICEF.

HELEN KELLER honored by **ELEANOR ROOSEVELT** at New York luncheon.

Margaret O'Brien

DR. ALBERT SCHWEITZER is awarded the most prestigious Order of Merit by **QUEEN ELIZABETH II**. With only 24 members, Dr. Schweitzer becomes the order's second living non-British honorary member.

TIME
Man of the Year
HARLOW CURTICE
(American Business Leader)

There She Is

Miss America
Lee Meriwether (California)

Miss Universe
Hillevi Rombi (Sweden)

Lee Meriwether

Hillevi Rombi

Danny Kaye

WHAT A YEAR IT WAS!

BIRTHDAYS BIRTHDAYS

THEY'RE JUST WILD ABOUT HARRY

Celebrating his 71st birthday in Independence, Missouri, former President **Harry S. Truman** is informed that he will be breaking ground for the new $1,750,000 Harry S. Truman Library. Declaring himself "fit as a fiddle," he later attends the annual Shrine Convention in Chicago wearing a fez and riding in the parade that lasts for seven hours.

BUILDING UP TO THIS

Celebrating his 88th birthday, architect **FRANK LLOYD WRIGHT** declares, "If I felt any better I couldn't stand it!"

Japan's **CROWN PRINCE AKIHITO** turns 21.

OLD AGE IS ALWAYS 15 YEARS AWAY

On turning 85, elder statesman **BERNARD BARUCH** quips, "To me, old age is always 15 years older than I am."

Silent-screen star **MARY PICKFORD** passes on a 62nd birthday celebration, saying "it takes time to grow old. I'm too busy. I have no time."

HAPPY BIRTHDAY, DEAR ALBIE

Over 500 people bearing flowers show up at **DR. ALBERT SCHWEITZER'S** hospital camp in the village of Lambarene in French Equatorial Africa to surprise him on his 80th birthday.

LADY CHURCHILL celebrates her 70th birthday in London.

Frank Lloyd Wright

Albert Schweitzer

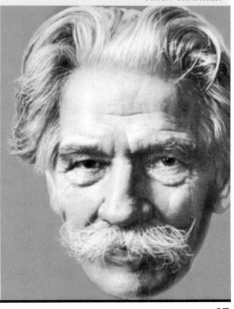

1955

Ills of the RICH & FAMOUS

From top: Bernard Baruch, Mamie Eisenhower, Susan Hayward, Lyndon Johnson

NEXT TIME TRY A BELLY FLOP

85-year-old **Bernard M. Baruch** hurts his hip trying to do a backflip in the swimming pool at his South Carolina estate.

BURNING THE CANDLE AT BOTH ENDS

Recovering from a bad bout with the flu, First Lady **Mamie Eisenhower** returns to the White House where her busy schedule wears her out quickly, forcing her to cancel all social engagements for a week.

TOO MANY BITTER PILLS TO SWALLOW

Rushed to the hospital for a stomach pumping, Hollywood actress **Susan Hayward** is recovering nicely after overdosing on sleeping pills at her San Fernando Valley home.

When told that she has a recurrence of her cancer, the world's greatest woman athlete **Babe Didrikson Zaharias** smiles and says, "Well, that's the rub of the green."

900 audience members get a refund as ailing **Eartha Kitt** leaves the stage during the 81st performance of *Mrs. Patterson*.

Babe Didrikson Zaharias, John F. Kennedy.

Senate Majority Leader **Lyndon B. Johnson** is discharged from Washington's Bethesda Naval Hospital where he has been recovering from a heart attack.

After a seven-month recuperation from spinal surgery to relieve an old World War II naval battle injury suffered when a Japanese destroyer sank the PT boat he commanded, Massachusetts' Democratic Senator **John F. Kennedy**, 38, returns to work.

WHAT A YEAR IT WAS!

ADMIRED ATTRACTIVE MEN

William Holden
John F. Kennedy
Edward R. Murrow
General Lauris Norstad
Gregory Peck

Gregory Peck

Edward R. Murrow

THEY PUT THEIR LIPS TOGETHER AND PUCKERED

Humphrey Bogart, 55, celebrates his 10th wedding anniversary with his beautiful wife, 30-year-old **Lauren Bacall**.

DID SHE GIVE HIM BACK THE RING?

Citing career conflicts, **Zsa Zsa Gabor's** mother, **Jolie**, announces the disengagement of her daughter from Dominican playboy **Porfirio Rubirosa**.

AN OFFSCREEN ROMANCE?

French actor **Jean-Pierre Aumont** romances **Grace Kelly** at the Cannes Film Festival.

IT'S NOT ABOUT THE MONEY, IT'S ABOUT THE MONEY

Following a $1 million divorce settlement from **Tyrone Power**, actress **Linda Christian** flies to London, saying "I didn't really want the million—it's all so taxable."

DO THEY VANT TO BE ALONE, DAHLING?

Dodging reporters, **Greta Garbo** arrives in Monte Carlo for a cruise to Saudi Arabia via Capri and Venice with Greek shipping magnate **Aristotle Onassis**.

Despite vacationing together in Boston, where they visited **Joe DiMaggio's** brother **Dom**, **Marilyn Monroe** denies that she and the former Yankee "slugger" are going to reconcile.

Coupling

Michael Caine & Patricia Haines

Alan Arkin & Jeremy Yaffe

Mike Wallace & Lorraine Perigord

Danny Aiello & Sandy Cohen

Bela Lugosi & Hope Lininger

Olivia de Havilland & Pierre Galante

Debbie Reynolds & Eddie Fisher

Betty Hutton & Alan Livingston

Orson Welles & Paola Mori

Ernie Kovacs & Edie Adams

Brian Keith & Judy Landon

Gregory Peck & Veronique Passani

Ray Charles & Della Howard

Buddy Hackett & Sherry Cohen

Jack Webb & Dorothy Towne

Sheree North & John M. Freeman

Clark Gable & Kay Williams Spreckels

Joan Crawford & Alfred N. Steele

Thurgood Marshall & Cecilia Suyat

Daniel Patrick Moynihan & Elizabeth Brennan

Joe Louis & Rose Morgan

Veronica Lake & Joseph A. McCarthy

Uncoupling

Edward G. Robinson & Gladys Lloyd Robinson

Margaret Leighton & Max Reinhardt

Ted Williams & Doris Soule Williams

Gloria Vanderbilt Stokowski & Leopold Stokowski

Rita Hayworth & Dick Haymes

Gregory Peck & Greta Kukkonen Peck

Sam Spiegel & Lynne Baggett

American women would grant divorces for six reasons:
- Physical or mental cruelty
- Excessive drinking
- Incompatibility
- Nonsupport
- Desertion
- Adultery

However, they would not grant a divorce for poor cooking or bad housekeeping. In addition, they strongly wanted a one-year forced wait before the ex-husband could remarry.

One of the greatest geniuses the world has ever seen died quietly in his sleep at age 76. German immigrant **ALBERT EINSTEIN** rewrote the basic scientific law of the universe. With the development of $E = mc^2$, Einstein proved mathematically that there can be no absolute measure of time or space because all spatial bodies are in perpetual motion relative to each other. He supported the Manhattan Project, which developed the atomic bomb. He felt morally compelled to produce the most destructive war tool the world had ever seen in response to the systematic destruction of the Jewish people, but later led scientists in urging an end to wars since "The Bomb" threatened humankind's continued existence.

Dale Carnegie, 66 Author and pioneer in public speaking and personality development, his book *How to Win Friends and Influence People* has sold over 10 million copies and has been translated into 29 languages since it was first published in 1936. An estimated 450,000 people worldwide have attended his courses, and he also wrote *How to Stop Worrying and Start Living*.

HUMAN INTEREST 1955

London's great central terminal

Queen Elizabeth II and the Duke of Edinburgh arrive for the formal inauguration of London airport's Great Central Terminal building.

With a terminal designed to accommodate an ever-increasing volume of passengers, the Queen hopes to maintain London's position as one of the great air travel centers of the world.

JULY 18

Walt Disney opens *DISNEYLAND*, a fantasyland for children of all ages, and welcomes its one millionth guest after only seven weeks.

1,243 European refugees arrive in New York by boat under the 1953 Immigration Act.

We're Big-City Folks

TWO OUT OF THREE PEOPLE in the United States can be classified as living in cities, where there is also a higher marriage ratio as well as a greater number of elderly people.

Only 13.5% of the U.S. population live on farms— down from 80% in the 1850s.

Get Out Those Toothpicks, Grandma CORN IS AMERICA'S NO. 1 FARM CROP.

in the west...
HILTON

Declaring "this will be the biggest hotel opening in the history of the business," Conrad Hilton opens his newest and plushest hotel, the $17 million, 450-room Beverly Hilton. The rooms will rent for as much as $65 a night.

in new york

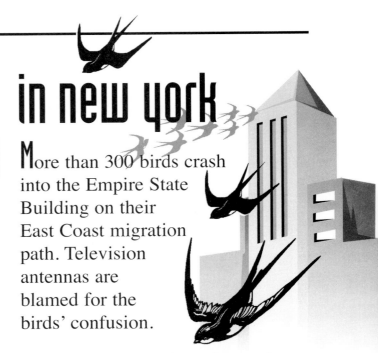

More than 300 birds crash into the Empire State Building on their East Coast migration path. Television antennas are blamed for the birds' confusion.

New York City has the greatest concentration of narcotic addicts in the U.S.

through a glass lightly...

New York's newest and biggest **Horn & Hardart Automat Cafeteria** opens on East 42nd Street. It boasts seating for 500 patrons and the "Finest Quality Food At Lowest Possible Prices."

WHAT A YEAR IT WAS!

Home Heating The Atomic Way

The Institute of Boiler & Radiator Manufacturers announces that American homes of the near future will be heated and cooled by small, economical atomic reactors. The new system will also provide unlimited hot water and melt snow from sidewalks and driveways.

Hot Time In The Old Town

For one historic hour, Arco, Idaho becomes the first small town to receive all its electricity from an experimental atomic power plant 20 miles away.

PUTTING YOUR CAN ON THE LINE

Every year the Canners League of America holds the California Cutting Bee, a gathering of manufacturers of canned food ranging from fruit cocktail to asparagus who have their food judged on appearance, quality, taste, texture, color and uniformity of product.

A POLL taken asks people what they thought life would be like in 20 years (1975). Here are some of the results:

- Push-button grocery selection which automatically assembles at checkout counter
- Food preservation using atomic rays
- Dirt-repellent fabrics
- Psychological counseling for babies
- Unconscious electric memorizer that allows you to record now and read later
- Mood detectors
- Mood-altering chemicals
- Ovens that cook food in seconds

a FAT chance

According to a recent study, fat at the dinner table does not necessarily turn into fat on the body, and in fact a diet high in fat helps promote beautiful skin, more energy, better bone development and better night vision.

THIS IS NO MOCKING MATTER

In a civil defense test, Operation Alert runs a three-day mock H-bomb drill in 53 U.S. cities that "results" in 8.5 million Americans dying and 2.5 million being evacuated while the government moves to 30 different shelters.

Citing that the H-bomb threatens man's *"continued existence,"* **ALBERT EINSTEIN** leads nine scientists to London to urge a ban on war.

There's a handy Kleenex package

for every tissue need!

LITTLE LULU says: For your convenience, there's a handy Kleenex* package to meet your every tissue need.

Choose Kleenex 200's, if that's the pack you like best. Or the new 400's Economy Pack in 3 lovely colors.

For bigger jobs, bigger blows, there's Jumbo Kleenex — the same strong, soft Kleenex tissues, only *bigger* (1 square foot). Jumbo, too, has the same exclusive "pop up" feature.

And when the family goes out, give them Kleenex Pocket Packs to go along. They fit neatly in purse or pocket. You can get a single Pack for only 5¢ and there's an extra saving when you buy the Bargain Bundle of 8 Kleenex Pocket Packs.

Be sure it's Kleenex

·the largest selling tissue in the world

firsts

A RACE AGAINST THE STORK

Mrs. Kathleen Foote of Axtell, Nebraska, the *first* woman elected to the Nebraska legislature since it became unicameral in 1934, goes into labor during a final vote on her *first* bill that would make it unlawful to throw trash on the highways.

CHICAGO'S O'HARE AIRPORT, named after America's greatest World War II naval hero, Edward "Butch" O'Hare, receives its *first* domestic flight.

THE BEECH PARIS, *first* executive jet plane, is displayed in Purchase, New York.

Col. Carlos Talbott flies cross-country in 3 hrs., 48 min. in the F-100C Super Sabre jet, the *first* supersonic combat plane.

FIRST SUBWAY TRAIN BEGINS RUNNING IN ROME.

The United States Air Force Academy in Colorado takes its *first* 306 cadets.

The U.S. Army commissions its *first* male nurse.

New **"DON'T WALK"** Signs Put Up At Busiest Intersections In New York.

The director of the Guinness brewing firm gives the green light to **Ross and Norris McWhirter** to compile their collection of offbeat information into the **Guinness Book of Superlatives.**

Universal Copyright Convention Goes Into Effect.

Church Of Scientology Founded By L. Ron Hubbard

The Presbyterian Church approves ordination of women.

OUTDOOR MOVIE THEATER HOSTS *FIRST* DRIVE-IN CHURCH SERVICE.

Sweeping away 5,000 years of Jewish tradition, Temple Avodah, a Reform Jewish congregation in Oceanside, Long Island, hires Mrs. Betty Robbins, a 31-year-old housewife from Massapequa, New York, to serve as their cantor during Rosh Hashanah, making her the *first* female cantor in Jewish history.

The opening of Parliament is televised in Canada for the *first* time.

WHAT A YEAR IT WAS!

the great move

IROQUOIS
WE HAVE TO GO BUT — WATCH US GROW
SPEED 30 MILES

In one of the greatest operations of its kind ever attempted, the entire town of Iroquois, Ontario, Canada is moved lock, stock and barrel to make way for the construction of the St. Lawrence Seaway.

JAS W. HARTSHORNE HOUSE MOVER

All 600 houses are moved without breaking so much as a dish.

Traffic Jam — Small Town U.S.A.

Hell No — But They're Forced To Go!

60,000 blacks demonstrate peacefully in South Africa to protest the government's plan to relocate minorities outside of Johannesburg. The first 130 black families are moved out by force to Meadowlands.

Now...

INSTANT OATMEAL

WITH **NEW** QUICK QUAKER OR MOTHER'S OATS

cooks creamy in 50-60 seconds

Something wonderful has happened to Quick Quaker Oats and Quick Mother's Oats.

Now — in just moments you have fully cooked oatmeal. Smoother oatmeal. Creamier. With the same full flavor — the same bountiful nourishment — of oatmeal that used to take hours of cooking.

These New Quick oat flakes — cut in tiny pieces — are rolled to a new tissue thinness. They cook in 50 to 60 seconds in boiling water.

So isn't it smart to eat a good hot oatmeal breakfast when it's quick as coffee? *New* Quick Quaker Oats and *New* Quick Mother's Oats are in stores now. Look for the Yellow Ribbon on the label.

All the protein nourishment of old fashioned oatmeal is present in this new, quick product. It helps keep adults fit—not fat, because it's so high in protein.

Best cereal for growing children. High-protein Quaker or Mother's Oats helps children grow strong bodies. Gives them stamina for school and play

QUAKER OATS

America's most popular cereal . . . hot or cold

Mother's Oats and Quaker Oats are exactly the same

CIVIL RIGHTS

CIVIL RIGHTS

COLOR BLIND

An all-white Methodist church in Old Mystic, Connecticut installs a black pastor.

Dora Lee Martin, a black student at the State University of Iowa, is named Iowa State Queen, beating out 29 white girls to become the first black coed to be awarded the crown.

Did The Good Ol' Boys Finally Put Away The Ropes?

The Tuskegee Institute reports that there have been no lynchings in the U.S. for three years.

ONE DRINKING FOUNTAIN FOR ALL

The Interstate Commerce Commission rules that racial segregation on interstate buses and trains and in terminals must end next year.

Roy Wilkins is named executive secretary of the NAACP.

Remember we are Fighting For Justice Do Not Ride A Bus Today

NEGRO BOYCOTT POSTER

This is one of the posters which city prisoners remember found from bus stop posts at Negroes stayed a boycott against the Montgomery City Lines over price.

ROSA PARKS is arrested in Montgomery, Alabama for refusing to give her seat to a white man, which kicks off the boycott of segregated buses led by Martin Luther King.

The U.S. Supreme Court renders its implementation decree reaffirming that segregation in public education is unconstitutional and orders the start toward desegregating public schools "with all deliberate speed." The controversial ruling affects more than 362 school districts and 134,000 black children. Strong resistance occurs in all but four southern states (Arkansas, Kentucky, Tennessee and Texas).

The court bans segregation in public parks, playgrounds and golf courses.

WHAT A YEAR IT WAS!

The SENATE 1955
The CONGRESS

The U.S. Senate votes 84-0 to continue loyalty inquiry in Civil Service.

Hawaiians
WANT STATEHOOD

A federal judge rules that Hawaii, a U.S. territory 2,091 miles from the mainland, is legally a "geographical part of the United States."

They Must Have Been
DEMOCRATS
THE U.S. CONGRESS votes to build 45,000 public housing units.

360 U.S. citizens petition the Supreme Court to ban the Internal Security Act of 1950.

U.S. Supreme Court upholds Massachusetts law banning adoption across religious lines.

SELECTIVE SERVICE EXTENDED UNTIL 1959.

THEY'RE SEEING STARS

The U.S. Congress introduces a resolution to bestow five-star Army general Douglas MacArthur the six-star honorary title of "General of the Armies of the United States."

ARE THEY AVAILABLE IN ROBIN'S NEST BLUE?

Hiring movie producer and director Cecil B. DeMille as his designer, Air Force Academy superintendent Lt. Gen. Hubert R. Harmon promises that his cadets will be the best-dressed men in military uniforms.

Called the largest peacetime army movement in U.S. history, the U.S. 10th Division from Fort Riley, Kansas arrives in Bremerhaven, Germany to replace the 1st Infantry Division in "Operation Gyroscope."

Another reason why he's

The best friend your car has ever had!

He sells top octane *Sky Chief* **with PETROX** for maximum **power** ... plus engine **protection!**

If you want to get *all* the power possible, and top engine protection *too* -- get Texaco Sky Chief gasoline. For Sky Chief and *only* Sky Chief has Petrox.

Petrox is unlike any other gasoline additive. It's an exclusive, petroleum-base element ... and contains no inorganic chemicals that can leave harmful deposits.

Petrox brings out maximum power, increases gasoline mileage — because it cuts deposits that *waste* power. What's more, Petrox leaves a fine film of protection on rings ... valves ... on about 123 parts in all. Result: up to 60% longer engine life. Millions of test-car miles *prove* it.

Prove it in *your* car. Fill up with top octane Sky Chief, supercharged with Petrox. The man to see is your Texaco Dealer, *the best friend your car has ever had.*

THE
TEXAS
COMPANY

TEXACO DEALERS in all 48 states
Texaco Products are also distributed in Canada and Latin America

TUNE IN ... TEXACO STAR THEATER starring DONALD O'CONNOR or JIMMY DURANTE on television, Saturday nights, NBC.

In Fort Worth, Texas, **BELL AIRCRAFT** displays a fixed-wing vertical takeoff plane.

Billed as *"the world's most popular airplane,"* Cessna introduces its **172 SKYHAWK**, a single-engine plane designed for the private pilot.

The **CHANCE VOUGHT F7U-3 CUTLASS** is the U.S. Navy's new jet fighter, and it's combat ready with air-to-air guided missiles.

A new speed record is set as a **BRITISH CANBERRA** jet is flown from London to New York in under 14.5 hours.

World's highest cable car introduced in Chamonix, France.

THE END OF THE LINE

New York's Third Avenue El ceases operations.

THE BRIDGED VERSION

The longest pipeline suspension bridge in the world is completed over the Mississippi River near Grand Tower, Illinois, and construction begins on the longest highway bridge in the world across Lake Pontchartrain in Louisiana.

NEW YORK STATE THRUWAY COMPLETED AS TAPPAN ZEE BRIDGE OPENS.

PAINTED SHOULDER LINES ON HIGHWAYS BEGIN AS EXPERIMENT IN WESTCHESTER COUNTY, NEW YORK.

WORLD'S DEEPEST CAUSEWAY OPENS, LINKING CAPE BRETON ISLAND TO NOVA SCOTIA MAINLAND.

69% OF THIS YEAR'S CARS WILL HAVE AUTOMATIC TRANSMISSIONS.

The hottest thing on wheels this year: the 1955 Chevy.

PROFILE
OF A TRAFFIC VIOLATOR

- ✓ Age between 21-25 years old
- ✓ Skilled or semiskilled worker
- ✓ Average intelligence
- ✓ Respect for the law
- ✓ Normal personality
- ✓ Good sense of humor
- ✓ One distinguishing feature: Breaks traffic laws and gets caught

ROAD RAGE
—The Early Years
A truck driver in Uniontown, Pennsylvania is arrested for firing his two pistols at approaching motorists who fail to dim their lights.

I Better Lay Off The Sauce — That Looks Like
A Moose
Patrons at a local pub in Anchorage are a bit startled as a moose sticks its head in the door, looks around and then leaves.

Is There A
FORD
In Your Future?
Members of the Ford family including Mrs. Edsel Ford, Henry Ford II, Benson Ford, Mr. & Mrs. William Clay Ford and Mrs. Walter Ford gather to dedicate the new $20 million, 17-story Henry Ford Hospital in Detroit.

1955

How Long's A Girl Supposed To Wait To Hit The Altar?

69-year-old Brit Fanny Ennis got tired of waiting around for her 73-year-old fiancé, John Purser, to marry her and she is suing him for breach of promise since he proposed to her in 1908.

How About Jumping In A Circle And Spinning Three Times?

The Indian Parliament passes the new Hindu Marriage Act to reform the 3,000-year-old Hindu law that allows a husband to dump his wife by simply saying, "Get thee to thy father's house. I will take another." Under the new law, Hindu women may now sue their husbands for divorce and collect alimony to boot, if they live a chaste life.

SHE'S NOT TAKING THIS WITHOUT A PEEP

A young bride in Italy complains to the police that her new husband forces her to wear a muzzle around the house to stop her from talking.

NAGGING WITHOUT WORDS IS STILL NAGGING

In Cleveland, a deaf-mute woman wins a divorce from her deaf-mute husband with the judge ruling "nagging in sign language can be just as effective as spoken words."

I'M JUST TRYING TO GET IT RIGHT, YOUR HONOR

A Navy man gets a quick annulment in Massachusetts after testifying that his wife concealed nine previous marriages.

A SURVEY

of 11,000 married couples reveals that one-third of all English men and women have not been in love by the time they reach 25.

Here are the qualities men and women are looking for in a mate:

GENTLEMEN:	LADIES:
BEAUTY	UNDERSTANDING
UNDERSTANDING	THOUGHTFULNESS
LOVE	SENSE OF HUMOR
FAITHFULNESS	INTEGRITY
	FAITHFULNESS

GET HER A BAGEL & CREAM CHEESE *immediately*

A large insurance company's breakfast survey of 1,600 Minneapolis white-collar workers reveals that 45% of women under 25 eat little or no break-fast while only 23% start their morning off with breakfast including juice, milk, egg or cereal. The survey reveals that the lack of breakfast affects the disposition and is bad for health and mental alertness.

Crimes & Misdemeanors

Crooks Are Stealing And Traders Aren't Trading

Some officials feel the lowest crime rate in 10 years during early October is due to the World Series, with the same reason credited for the slump in the New York Stock Exchange.

Five days after it is stolen from the British Museum, Scotland Yard sleuths find the Strasbourg manuscript of "La Marseillaise," one of only three original copies of the French national anthem in existence.

That Ain't No J•O•K•E

The Board of Supervisors bans the sale of violent comic books in Los Angeles.

Murder, Inc. "executioner" Albert Anastasia pleads guilty to income tax evasion as a search is made for key prosecution witness Charles Ferri.

N.Y.C. POLICE
57939
10 22 36

Is There Such A Thing As "An Accident"?

Instead of reading "You need a *friend* in the City Council," the ad read "You need a *fiend* in the City Council," and candidate for Los Angeles City Council Sam Schulman is suing THE WILSHIRE PRESS for negligence.

postal news

POST OFFICE TO TEST BALLPOINT PENS TO SEE HOW MANY ARE STOLEN

The U.S. Post Office announces it will test 20,000 ballpoint pens that will be chained to desks to determine how they stand up and how many are stolen.

President Eisenhower vetoes 8.8% pay increase for postal workers but subsequently approves an 8% increase.

Proof of Delivery

The U.S. Post Office introduces certified mail, which requires the recipient to sign a receipt as proof of delivery.

"Occupant" now appears on envelopes sent by advertisers after the U.S. Post Office announces it will no longer deliver unaddressed mail.

WHAT A YEAR IT WAS!

1955

a meteoric crawl to fame

A giant tortoise alive and crawling at 177 years old is still the household pet of the royal family of Tongatabu, principal island of the Tonga group.

it's a dog's life

No. of Americans Who Own Dogs
23,000,000

Amount of Money Spent on Dog Food Annually
$200,000,000

"And The Little Dog Shall Lead Him"

Magazine and calendar dog supermodel, Butch, a black and white cocker spaniel who lost his sight to cataracts, is seen being led into a Christmas sale for the blind by his son, Butch Jr., who acts as his "seeing eye dog."

a dog by any other name… The American Kennel Club announces that the Lhasa apso dog will no longer be classified as a terrier.

Maybe He Should Switch To Guard Monkeys?

A veterinarian in Pasadena, California reports that a thief broke into his office and made off with $50 while 30 of his resident dogs snoozed away.

animal corner

$E = mc^2$

Psychologist/animal trainer Keller B. Breland concludes that pigs are the most intelligent animals, followed by raccoons, dogs and cats. Horses and cows rank low on the intelligence scale, while hens have been taught to play baseball, poker and walk on a tightrope.

THE CARE OF YOUR PUSSY

Research on the nutritional needs of cats conducted at Rutgers University concludes that cats, like humans, require personal attention and affection, and fondling before mealtime will contribute to their psychological well-being and enhance their appetites.

THIS IS ONE FOR THE BIRDS

Adding to his list of "#1 titles," Juan Perón is named Argentina's #1 canary breeder.

Canary Team Musical Champs

The Roller Canary Contest of Greater New York is won by a team of four canaries beating out 54 other competing singing teams.

and a partridge in a pear tree

The Nativity scene at New York's Botanical Garden gets a bit crowded when twin lambs born to one of four Dorset ewes join a goat and six chickens. Reportedly, the other three ewes are also in a family way, but no "ewe" date is announced.

WHAT A YEAR IT WAS!

THAT IS ONE SEXY SET OF BONES

Michigan chiropractors study X-rays from dozens of candidates vying for the Posture Queen of 1955 title to determine who has the best intervertebral fibro-cartilages.

A bust of the last survivor of the Union army, Albert Woolson, is unveiled in Duluth, Minnesota to celebrate his 108th birthday.

One Of George's Many Beds

Four Virginia ladies, descendants of General Robert E. Lee, donate a linen campaign tent that served as a sleeping shelter for General George Washington to the National Park Service, which will house it in a historical park in Yorktown, Virginia.

GERMAN ARCHAEOLOGISTS FIND MOLDS USED TO CAST THE GIANT SCULPTURE OF ZEUS.

With the Italian Navy scheduled to do the dredging, plans are being made in Syracuse, Sicily to recover 119 ships that were part of the Athenian fleet of 134 ships that sank in 413 B.C.

Israel purchases the Dead Sea Scrolls from the Syrian archbishop metropolitan in Jerusalem for a reported $250,000.

EXPLORING NEW FRONTIERS

A BREATHTAKING EXPERIENCE

A British climbing party scales Mt. Kanchenjunga in the Himalayas, the world's third-highest peak as well as the highest unclimbed peak.

Rear Admiral Richard E. Byrd leads U.S. Antarctic expedition and is eventually placed in charge of all U.S. activities in that region.

1955

FOREIGN

The Greening Of The Negev

Israeli President Itzhak Ben-Zvi presses a lever and the floodgates open as giant diesel pumps begin to send water from the Yarkon River into a pipeline that goes to the Negev Desert.

OIL IS DISCOVERED IN ISRAEL IN THE NEGEV AREA.

Peru grants women voting rights.

Freedom of worship becomes law in Hanoi.

58 passengers are killed when an Israeli airliner is downed in Bulgaria.

At the end of his 10-year term as French Ambassador to the United States—"the happiest years of my life"—**Henri Bonnet** is bid a fond adieu by friends, including Marlene Dietrich, as he sails back to France.

THE VATICAN orders Britain's Roman Catholics to quit the Council of Christians and Jews, stating membership would cause Catholics to regard their religion as no more valid than any other.

Sir Winston Churchill, the only surviving member of the Big Three (which also included Joseph Stalin and Franklin D. Roosevelt), lambasts the version of the Yalta secret documents published in the U.S., calling them filled with serious mistakes.

THE BIG CHILL

Blizzards, gale-force winds and severe flooding devastate Europe.

AFFAIRS

1955

25 JAPANESE WOMEN,
VICTIMS OF HIROSHIMA, ARRIVE IN AMERICA
FOR PLASTIC SURGERY TO BE PERFORMED AT
NEW YORK'S MOUNT SINAI HOSPITAL.

JAPAN AND KOREA
DISPUTE FISHING RIGHTS

Hundreds of Japanese fishermen converge on the Korean diplomatic mission to protest against their exclusion from international fishing grounds claimed by Korea.

Korean Diplomatic Mission in Japan

With the Korean navy under orders to shoot to sink, a nasty crisis grows steadily worse, aggravating the two countries' already bad relationship — a continuing problem since war's end.

Representatives of the fishermen meet Korean diplomats to state grievances as they are now cut off from some of the richest waters, severely impacting on Japan's fishing industry.

WHAT A YEAR IT WAS!

59

A TOBACCO COUNCIL representative, trying to invalidate "implied" meaning in a U.S. government report, claims that cigarette smoking has declined due to high sales taxes, not because of health fears.

THE DRINKING SCORE

1. France
2. Italy
3. Switzerland
4. Great Britain
5. United States
6. West Germany

PASSINGS

CHIEF IRON HAIL, Approx. 98
The last survivor of the Battle of Little Big Horn, 1876.

IRA HAYES, 32
An American Indian, Hayes was one of the marines who raised the American flag at Iwo Jima during World War II.

JANE HERVEUX, Approx. 65
The first female to fly a plane solo.

HAMMOND FISHER, 55
Creator of the comic strip "Joe Palooka," read by approximately 50 million people every day.

U.S. STATISTICS

COUPLING & UNCOUPLING

MARRIAGES: 1,531,000	DIVORCES: 370,000 *(approx.)*

ARRIVALS

BIRTHS: 4,097,000

What Ever Happened To
"SEE SPOT RUN"?
A national furor erupts over a syndicated version of Rudolf Flesch's best-selling book, *Why Johnny Can't Read*, an indictment of the educational system's failure to teach children to read as a result of abandoning phonics in favor of sight recognition.

There are approximately 8,240 public libraries in the U.S.

Now Let's See What They'll Do With
Mississippi
With 152 variations, the word "question" is the word most misspelled by elementary school children.

WHAT A YEAR IT WAS!

New Words & Expressions

A-Line
A feminine fashion featuring a flared skirt that tends to give the wearer the silhouette of an "A"

Skymobile
A helicopter

Soap-Sudder
A writer and producer of TV shows

Brush Fire War
A small but dangerous war

Space Divider
A cabinet unit or partial wall used to divide areas of a house

Church Key
A can or bottle opener used for opening beer

Toll TV
Television paid for by the viewer with a metering device

ICBM
(formerly IBM) Intercontinental Ballistic Missile

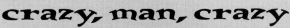

Water Barrier
A speed of about 200 mph, considered very difficult for speedboats to attain or exceed

Pedestrian Window
A teller's window placed on the outside of a bank so that depositors can do business without going inside

Rock and Roll
A dance to music heavily accented on the second and fourth beats

crazy, man, crazy

Americans are fascinated with the bohemian clothes, colorful language and use of marijuana associated with the **"beat generation,"** whose alienated-from-society writers include **Jack Kerouac**, **William Burroughs** and **Allen Ginsberg**.

when steel goes to work in your office . . .

. . . it gives your company continuing dividends in efficient, strong, long-lasting office equipment, pleasant surroundings and satisfied personnel.

People are proud to work in offices made attractive by steel. With machines made of steel they can turn out more work faster, with little effort.

Many tons of J&L Steels are fabricated yearly into office equipment. Manufacturers use J&L Sheet and Strip Steel for movable wall partitions, desks, file cabinets, and the housings of business machines. J&L Cold Finished Steels are fashioned into the smooth-working parts of the machines.

J&L Sheet and Strip and J&L Cold Finished Steels are fine-quality steels, supplied to the specifications of manufacturers of a great variety of office equipment.

Jones & Laughlin
STEEL CORPORATION — *Pittsburgh*

Hot and Cold Rolled Sheet and Strip • Tin Plate • Tubular Products • Plates, Structurals, Hot Rolled Bars • Hot Extruded and Cold Drawn Bars • Wire and Wire Products Alloy Products • Electricweld Tubing • Wire Rope • Steel Containers • Coal Chemicals

Look to J & L . . . for the steels that work for modern industry

Arts & ENTERTAINMENT

MOVIES

Jean Simmons and Marlon Brando

BRANDO CLEANS UP HIS ACT FOR *GUYS AND DOLLS*

Starring as *Guys and Dolls* gambler Sky Masterson, **Marlon Brando** trades in his motorcycle duds for a slick, dapper wardrobe and sings and dances into a spotlight of a different color.

MUSIC

THAR'S GOLD IN THEM THAR SONGS

Released on more than 20 different labels, **Davy Crockett** songs sell an estimated seven million copies in less than six months.

TELEVISION

COLOR TV BECOMES MORE ACCESSIBLE

RCA simplifies 21" home color receiver. Advances in standardization and production contribute to growth in color television.

WHAT A YEAR IT WAS!

ART

The market for modern art soars as price tags for works by **Kandinsky**, **Mondrian** and **Klee** increase dramatically.

Paul Klee drawing

What's Playing AT THE MOVIES

Cinerama Holiday

DADDY LONG LEGS

THE DESPERATE HOURS

DIABOLIQUE

EAST OF EDEN

The Glass Slipper

GUYS AND DOLLS

HIT THE DECK

I Am A Camera

I'll Cry Tomorrow

Interrupted Melody

It Came From Beneath The Sea

It's Always Fair Weather

KISMET

Lady And The Tramp

THE LADYKILLERS

The Left Hand Of God

**ABBOTT AND COSTELLO
MEET THE MUMMY**

Ain't Misbehavin'

Artists And Models

BAD DAY AT BLACK ROCK

BATTLE CRY

THE BIG KNIFE

BLACKBOARD JUNGLE

The Bridges At Toko-Ri

LOLA MONTES

The Long Gray Line

Love Is A Many-Splendored Thing

Love Me Or Leave Me

A Man Called Peter

THE MAN FROM LARAMIE

The Man With The Golden Arm

Many Rivers To Cross

MARTY

MISTER ROBERTS

My Sister Eileen

The Night Of The Hunter

NOT AS A STRANGER

OKLAHOMA!

Pete Kelly's Blues

Picnic

The Prodigal

Queen Bee

REBEL WITHOUT A CAUSE

RICHARD III

The Rose Tattoo

The Seven Little Foys

THE SEVEN YEAR ITCH

STRATEGIC AIR COMMAND

SUMMERTIME

THE TENDER TRAP

This Island Earth

To Catch A Thief

TO HELL AND BACK

The Trouble With Harry

The Virgin Queen

WE'RE NO ANGELS

You're Never Too Young

1955

Jane Wyman & Ross Hunter

Rock Hudson & Connie Worcher

Mr. & Mrs. Jeff Chandler

ACADEMY AWARDS CEREMONY

Held on March 30, 1955

Marlon Brando accepts Best Actor award for his 1954 performance in *On the Waterfront*.

Presenter Bette Davis wears a special "space helmet" as she shaved her head for role as Queen Elizabeth I in *The Virgin Queen*.

Grace Kelly receives Best Actress award from William Holden for her 1954 performance in *The Country Girl*.

WHAT A YEAR IT WAS!

The Academy Awards

"And The Winner Is..."

Bob Hope *hosts the* Academy Awards *on the* West Coast *and* Thelma Ritter *hosts on the* East Coast.

Oscars® Presented in 1955

BEST PICTURE
ON THE WATERFRONT

BEST ACTOR
MARLON BRANDO, *On The Waterfront*

BEST ACTRESS
GRACE KELLY, *The Country Girl*

BEST DIRECTOR
ELIA KAZAN, *On The Waterfront*

BEST SUPPORTING ACTOR
EDMOND O'BRIEN, *The Barefoot Contessa*

BEST SUPPORTING ACTRESS
EVA MARIE SAINT, *On The Waterfront*

BEST SONG
"THREE COINS IN THE FOUNTAIN"

Grace Kelly

1955 Favorites *(Oscars® Presented in 1956)*

BEST PICTURE
MARTY

BEST ACTOR
ERNEST BORGNINE, *Marty*

BEST ACTRESS
ANNA MAGNANI, *The Rose Tattoo*

BEST DIRECTOR
DELBERT MANN, *Marty*

BEST SUPPORTING ACTOR
JACK LEMMON, *Mr. Roberts*

BEST SUPPORTING ACTRESS
JO VAN FLEET, *East Of Eden*

BEST SONG
"LOVE IS A MANY SPLENDORED THING"

Ernest Borgnine

1955

BIG BUCKS AT THE BOX OFFICE

June Allyson
Humphrey Bogart
Marlon Brando
Gary Cooper
Clark Gable
William Holden
Grace Kelly
Dean Martin &
Jerry Lewis
James Stewart
John Wayne

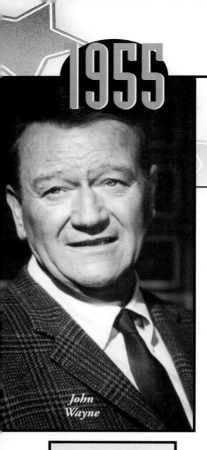

John Wayne

SOME LIKE IT HOT

Drive-in movie theaters are enjoying year-round business thanks to a portable electric heater for the floor of your car that you can rent for 25¢.

STARS OF TOMORROW

Ernest Borgnine
James Dean
Richard Egan
Anne Francis
Tab Hunter
Jack Lemmon
Dorothy Malone
Kim Novak
Eva Marie Saint
Russ Tamblyn

TOP BUCKS AT THE BOX OFFICE

Cinerama Holiday

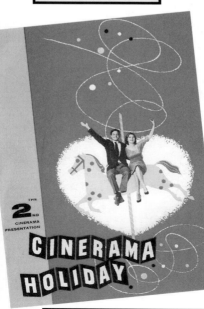

2ND CINERAMA PRESENTATION

CINERAMA HOLIDAY

Marlon Brando and Eva Marie Saint

ON THE WATERFRONT TRIVIA

✓ First film in which a character says *"Go to hell."*

✓ Ties the 8-Oscar record set by *Gone with the Wind* in 1939 and matched by *From Here to Eternity* in 1953.

✓ Every major studio in Hollywood turned down the original script.

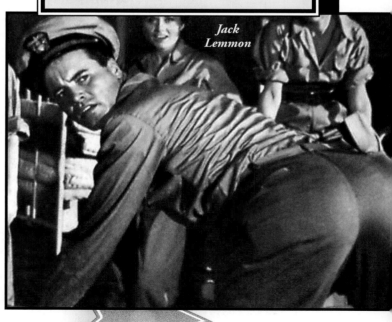

Jack Lemmon

A DAY AT THE CIRCUS

Top stars turn out for the opening night of Ringling Brothers Barnum & Bailey circus at Madison Square Garden to benefit the Arthritis & Rheumatism Foundation.

Martha Raye hams it up with a funny face.

Milton Berle lends his talents as ringmaster of this glittering extravaganza called "Rainbow 'Round the World."

Jimmy Cagney waves to the enthusiastic crowd.

Marilyn Monroe rides a pink elephant, adding to the excitement.

The long-awaited *Benny Goodman Story* gets its first public screenings at special "by invitation only" press previews in New York and major cities across the nation. The film depicts Benny Goodman's rise from a Chicago tenement to Carnegie Hall and national fame.

Steve Allen and his wife, **Jayne Meadows**, attend the premiere of *The Benny Goodman Story*.

Leading motion picture executives and celebrities turn out to attend this tribute to the "King of Swing" starring Steve Allen.

Benny Goodman, Allen and Meadows congratulate each other.

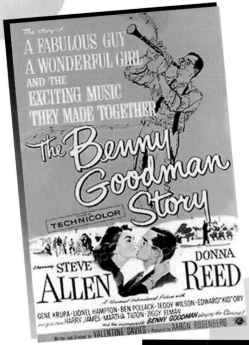

WHAT A YEAR IT WAS!

ROCK HUDSON receives *Modern Screen* award for Most Popular Actor for second year in a row.

Kirk Douglas (left) and Rock Hudson

SCREEN DEBUTS

Dennis Hopper in *Rebel Without a Cause.*

Cloris Leachman in **Robert Aldrich's** landmark film noir, *Kiss Me Deadly.*

Shirley MacLaine in **Alfred Hitchcock's** black comedy, *The Trouble with Harry.*

Dancer **Jill Ireland** in *Oh, Rosalinda!!*

Blake Edwards writes the screenplay *My Sister Eileen* and makes his directorial debut with *Bring Your Smile Along.*

Shirley MacLaine

Bob Fosse choreographs his first film, *My Sister Eileen.*

While filming Hitchcock's *To Catch a Thief* on the French Riviera, **Grace Kelly** meets **Prince Rainier** of Monaco.

★ famous births

Isabelle Adjani	Glenne Headly
Sandra Bernhard	Margaux Hemingway
Edgar Bronfman Jr.	Gale Anne Hurd
Dana Carvey	Ray Liotta
Kevin Costner	Bill Paxton
Willem Dafoe	Paul Rodriguez
Jeff Daniels	Gary Sinise
Judy Davis	Billy Bob Thornton
Griffin Dunne	Bruce Willis
Roland Emmerich	Debra Winger
Whoopi Goldberg	Steven Wright

MULE SKINNER BLUES

With **Francis the Talking Mule** racking up most of the fan mail, **Donald O'Connor** leaves the successful "Francis" series to move on to other pastures.

FRANCIS GOES TO THE RACES

Starring
DONALD O'CONNOR
PIPER LAURIE
and
FRANCIS
the Talking Mule
with CECIL KELLAWAY
JESSE WHITE

PASSINGS

THEDA BARA, 69
"Vamp" star of silent films, including *The She-Devil, Cleopatra* and *The Vixen,* Bara was forbidden to marry and appear in public without a veil while under contract with Fox.

JAMES DEAN, 24
One of Hollywood's most popular and handsome actors, James Dean is killed after hitting another car with his Porsche Spyder. With the success of his films *East of Eden, Rebel Without a Cause* and *Giant,* Dean, who often portrayed restless characters, became a favorite of disenfranchised youth across the nation. Before his film career, Dean appeared in *The Immoralist* on Broadway, earning him both a Bloom Award for Best Newcomer and the opportunity to work in Hollywood.

SHEMP HOWARD, 60
Along with brothers Moe and Curly, Brooklyn-born Shemp was a member of the Three Stooges comedy team, famous for their slapstick humor.

CARMEN MIRANDA, 46
Colorful Brazilian film star of the 1940s known as "The Brazilian Bombshell," Lisbon-born Maria do Carmo Miranda Da Cunha was as famous for her dancing and singing as she was for her colorful hats decorated with fruit. Her first major American film was *Down Argentine Way,* and at one time she was the highest-paid performer in the U.S.

ROBERT RISKIN, 58
Screenwriter of such classic films as *Lost Horizon, It Happened One Night* and *You Can't Take It With You,* Riskin worked for the Office of War Information during World War II.

Theda Bara

Carmen Miranda

Betty Hutton announces that being a full-time mom just isn't enough to keep her busy, so she's coming out of retirement and back into show business.

QUE BELLA
The most photographed star at the International Film Festival in Cannes this year is **Sophia Loren**.

Enrico Caruso's family finds the portrayal of the great tenor in MGM's film *The Great Caruso* insulting to the honor of the family and collects $8,300 in damages from the studio.

Marilyn Monroe tells newsmen at a Third Avenue bar that she wants to put more emphasis on sophistication and less on sex in her movies.

Starring in his own screen biography, **Nat "King" Cole** quips that "dialogue is just lyrics that don't rhyme."

SO MAYBE SHE DOES VANT TO BE ALONE
Fourteen years after her last film, the Academy honors Greta Garbo who, you guessed it, was a no-show.

Bing Crosby begins shooting his 50th picture—a remake of *Anything Goes*.

ART IMITATES LIFE
World War II Air Force colonel, actor **James Stewart**, is cast in *The Spirit of St. Louis*, the story of **Charles A. Lindbergh**.

FLASHING THOSE PEARLY WHITES
Liberace stars in his first film, *Sincerely Yours*.

¿DÓNDE ESTÁ EL GATO?
Warner Bros.' animation studio launches **Speedy Gonzales**, "The Fastest Mouse in All of Mexico."

DOCTOR IN THE HOUSE
Olivia de Havilland costars with **Robert Mitchum** as the devoted, long-suffering wife in *Not As a Stranger*, the film based on the best-selling book.

Greta Garbo

Bing Crosby

WHAT A YEAR IT WAS!

motion picture that ran a year on Broadway at $3.50!

RODGERS & HAMMERSTEIN present **OKLAHOMA!**

Color by TECHNICOLOR

CinemaScope

starring

GORDON MacRAE · GLORIA GRAHAME
SHIRLEY JONES · GENE NELSON
CHARLOTTE GREENWOOD
EDDIE ALBERT · JAMES WHITMORE
ROD STEIGER

Music by RICHARD RODGERS · Book & Lyrics by OSCAR HAMMERSTEIN II
Screenplay by SONYA LEVIEN and WILLIAM LUDWIG · Dances Staged by AGNES DE MILLE
Produced by ARTHUR HORNBLOW, JR. · Directed by FRED ZINNEMANN
A MAGNA PRODUCTION · DISTRIBUTED BY 20th CENTURY-FOX

OKLAHOMA! "THE FILM"

Oklahoma!, the world's most successful musical comedy, opens to critical acclaim, utilizing the new Todd-AO process with its specially engineered wide-angle lenses and film almost double regular movie size.

20th Century Fox begins shooting its first SuperCinemaScope film.

RKO SELLS LIBRARY TO TV INDUSTRY

Despite Hollywood's "unofficial" policy of disregarding the television industry, **Howard Hughes** sells the RKO film library for television distribution.

After a six-year court battle, **Sam Goldwyn** outbids "America's Sweetheart" **Mary Pickford** and wins ownership of United Artists studio.

AND THE ROCKETTES, TOO

Kismet opens at Radio City Music Hall.

CARVED IN CEMENT

The Hollywood Chamber of Commerce votes to add multicolored squares of pavement to be set into sidewalks around Hollywood and Vine which will be used to embed the profiles of movie, radio, television and recording stars.

BUT WHAT ABOUT THE BREASTS AT LES FOLIES BERGERE?

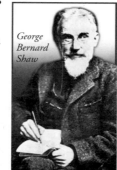

George Bernard Shaw

The puritanical leaders of the famed Comédie-Française ban a production of **George Bernard Shaw's** play *Mrs. Warren's Profession* on the grounds that Mrs. Warren is "amoral," and her saga "very bad and boring."

WHOOPS, THERE'S THAT BLUE PENCIL AGAIN

Great Britain bans *The Blackboard Jungle*.

UA RESIGNS FROM MPAA OVER RATINGS

The Man with the Golden Arm opens to rave reviews despite the MPAA's failure to grant its seal of approval, and United Artists resigns from the association as its way of lodging a strong protest.

FRANK SINATRA · ELEANOR PARKER · KIM NOVAK

THE MAN WITH THE GOLDEN ARM

A FILM BY OTTO PREMINGER

Now, for '55 Motorola TV introduces the

BIG LOOK

17"
TABLE MODEL
$129⁹⁵

21"
TABLE MODEL
$149⁹⁵

21"
CONSOLE
$199⁹⁵

NEW BIG LOOK PICTURE

with Giant "Extended Area" Screen – World's Largest!

Motorola's BIG LOOK, size for size, gives you the biggest picture ever achieved on any television screen! A *brighter* picture, too, with new alumi- nized tube. Motorola's Lifetime Focus never needs adjusting keeps picture quality sharp and clear. Better see the big difference the BIG LOOK makes!

BIG LOOK PERFORMANCE

with new, bigger, stronger '55 Power-Drive Chassis!

Here's Motorola's sensational new Power-Drive chassis. Radically ad- vanced, with stepped-up signal pulling power. Brings in sharper, stronger, BIG LOOK pictures. New Automatic Pic- ture Control keeps them steadily clear, contrasty, brilliant. It's the dependable performance only Motorola can give!

PLUS MODERN/SLANT STYLING!

Only Motorola TV gives the combined advantages of new BIG LOOK picture, new decorator-styled cabinetry, *plus* new Glare Down/Sound Up design! See at right how the tinted Glare Guard screen deflects glare *down* how the tilted Golden Voice speaker directs sound *up!* See why new BIG LOOK Motorola TV is the BIG BUY in modern television!

GLARE·DOWN
FOR CLEARER PICTURE

SOUND·UP
FOR CLEARER TONE

Better See
Motorola TV

What's New On TV

The Adventures Of Robin Hood

The Alcoa Hour

Alfred Hitchcock Presents

The Amazing Dunninger

America's Greatest Bands

And Here's The Show

Are Husbands Really Necessary?

Around The World With Orson Welles

The Big Surprise

Brave Eagle

Captain Kangaroo

Casablanca

Cheyenne

The Crusader

Dr. Hudson's Secret Journal

The Eddie Cantor Comedy Theater

Ford Star Jubilee

Frankie Laine Time

The Grand Ole Opry

Gunsmoke

Highway Patrol

The Honeymooners

It's Always Jan

Jan Murray Time

The Johnny Carson Show

Jungle Jim

King's Row

The Lawrence Welk Show

The Life And Legend Of Wyatt Earp

The Martha Raye Show

The Millionaire

Norby (first series filmed in color)

The Orson Welles Sketchbook

Ozark Jubilee

The People's Choice

The Phil Silvers Show

Sergeant Preston Of The Yukon

Sheena: Queen Of The Jungle

The $64,000 Question

The Soupy Sales Show

Spotlight Playhouse

Wonderama

ABC-TV, still broadcasting in black and white, launches two Disney programs—*Disneyland*, the highest-rated evening program for children, and *The Mickey Mouse Club*, which reaches an audience of up to 10 million every afternoon.

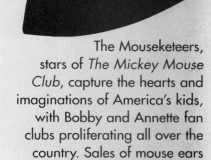

The Mouseketeers, stars of *The Mickey Mouse Club*, capture the hearts and imaginations of America's kids, with Bobby and Annette fan clubs proliferating all over the country. Sales of mouse ears reach 26,000 weekly during the height of "Mickey mania."

TOP TEN TELEVISION SHOWS

The **George Gobel Show**
I Love Lucy
The **Jackie Gleason Show**
Disneyland
Ford Theater
Dragnet
Toast Of The Town
Producers' Showcase
Lux Video Theatre
Your Hit Parade

TOP TV PROGRAMS [WINTER]

I Love Lucy
The **Jackie Gleason Show**
You Bet Your Life
Dragnet
Disneyland
The **Milton Berle Show**
The **Martha Raye Show**
The **Colgate Comedy Hour**
Toast Of The Town

TOP TV PROGRAMS [SUMMER]

$64,000 Question
Toast Of The Town
Dragnet
Climax
Miss America Pageant
Lux Video Theatre
Two For The Money
Gunsmoke
Disneyland
Undercurrent

Television Firsts

- First televised presidential press conference.
- First popular song to win an Emmy: **Frank Sinatra's** "Love and Marriage."
- First color broadcast of the World Series is televised by NBC.
- First network animated series, *Mighty Mouse Playhouse*, premieres on CBS.
- First overseas broadcast from Havana to Miami.
- First televised Emmy Awards, **Steve Allen** hosting.
- First commercial television broadcasts in Britain.

Peter Pan, starring **Mary Martin**, tops the ratings for NBC, with 65 million viewers tuning in.

The Lawrence Welk Show, a new series, is panned by *TV Guide*.

CBS introduces *The Johnny Carson Show*.

CBS introduces **Bob Keeshan** (formerly Clarabell the Clown) as *Captain Kangaroo*.

Gunsmoke, popular on radio since 1952, makes its debut on TV.

Du Mont TV network shuts down due to financial losses.

Disneyland

From top: Steve Allen, Lucille Ball, Jackie Gleason

WHAT A YEAR IT WAS!

Jack Benny (left) and Johnny Carson

TV BLUES

Disgruntled with the quality of television programming, producer **Fred Coe** warns that TV will "become the nation's next drug."

Pocket-size, battery-operated radios introduced.

"Pay-as-you-see" television receives mixed reviews as heated discussions reflect pro and con views around this new concept.

OTHER FAVORITES

The Big Surprise

Max Liebman Presents

Captain Kangaroo

Norby

Dear Phoebe

The Phil Silvers Show

Studio One

The Groucho Marx Show

Ponds Theatre

Omnibus

The Jack Benny Show

Professional Father

Truth or Consequences

Lassie

The Adventures of Rin Tin Tin

Your Hit Parade

CAPTAIN VIDEO CANCELLED

Wearers of the Captain Video decoder ring are dismayed when their favorite interplanetary show, *Captain Video*, is given the ax after a seven-year run.

Dave Garroway continues hosting the revolutionary magazine format *Today* show, over which he's presided since **Pat Weaver** created the concept in 1952.

TV COUPLES

Lucy & Desi
Jack Paar & Edie Adams
Garry Moore & Denise Lor
George Gobel & Peggy King

Number of TV sets in America: 33.5 million

BIG-JACKPOT QUIZ SHOWS

The $64,000 Question

The Big Surprise

Stop The Music

Hal March, host of The $64,000 Question

WHAT A YEAR IT WAS!

BEHIND THE SCREEN

Early Warner Bros. cartoons, including **Daffy Duck** and **Porky Pig**, can now be seen under the umbrella title *Looney Tunes*.

Ed Sullivan

Frank Sinatra gets into a dispute with **Ed Sullivan** when he refuses to appear on *The Ed Sullivan Show* gratis to plug his new film *Guys and Dolls*.

SHARPENING THE BLACK & WHITE
General Electric Co. has developed an improved color broadcasting method assuring a sharp monochrome picture when the program is being televised in color.

NBC dramatically increases color broadcasting.

THE DAWN OF THE COUCH POTATO
Zenith Radio demonstrates a new kind of television set that uses a flash beam (electric eye) from a small, wireless, handheld gadget that turns the set on and changes channels.

DON'T GET UP CLOSE AND TOO PERSONAL
According to a report issued by the National Society for Prevention of Blindness, watching television does not harm the eyes if you follow these guidelines:

- Make sure the picture is in clear focus.
- Use soft, indirect light.
- Never watch TV in a totally dark room.
- Sit as far from the screen as possible.

THEY DON'T CALL IT THE "BOOB TUBE" FOR NOTHING
A Northwestern University study on children's television habits reveals the following:

- Children between the ages of 8 and 13 spend over 20 hours a week watching television.
- Children in the upper fourth of their class are found to spend 20 hours a week watching television while children in the lower fourth spend up to 26 hours.
- Excessive time in front of the television can result in such symptoms as eyestrain, fatigue, nervousness, less interest in playing and loss of interest in school.

Ed McConnell   Andy Devine

BUSTER BROWN

AND NOW FOR A VERY SPECIAL SHOE
Smilin' Ed McConnell and His Buster Brown Gang returns to the air as *Andy's Gang* hosted by **Andy Devine**.

FAMOUS BIRTHS

Nina **Blackwood**
Peter **Gallagher**
Kelsey **Grammer**
David Alan **Grier**
Arsenio **Hall**
Penn **Jillette**
Jane **Kaczmarek**
Howie **Mandel**
Laurie **Metcalf**
Kate **Mulgrew**
Bill **Nye**
Connie **Sellecca**
Maria **Shriver**
Jimmy **Smits**
Greta **Van Susteren**

WHAT A YEAR IT WAS!

EMMY awards

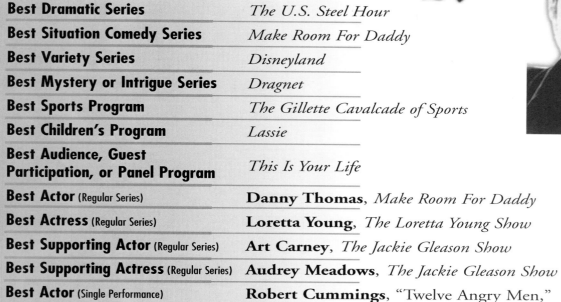

Best Dramatic Series	*The U.S. Steel Hour*
Best Situation Comedy Series	*Make Room For Daddy*
Best Variety Series	*Disneyland*
Best Mystery or Intrigue Series	*Dragnet*
Best Sports Program	*The Gillette Cavalcade of Sports*
Best Children's Program	*Lassie*
Best Audience, Guest Participation, or Panel Program	*This Is Your Life*
Best Actor (Regular Series)	**Danny Thomas**, *Make Room For Daddy*
Best Actress (Regular Series)	**Loretta Young**, *The Loretta Young Show*
Best Supporting Actor (Regular Series)	**Art Carney**, *The Jackie Gleason Show*
Best Supporting Actress (Regular Series)	**Audrey Meadows**, *The Jackie Gleason Show*
Best Actor (Single Performance)	**Robert Cummings**, "Twelve Angry Men," *Studio One*
Best Actress (Single Performance)	**Judith Anderson**, "Macbeth," *Hallmark Hall of Fame*
Best Male Singer	**Perry Como**
Best Female Singer	**Dinah Shore**
Best News Reporter	**John Daly**
Most Outstanding New Personality	**George Gobel**
Best Written Dramatic Material	**Reginald Rose**, "Twelve Angry Men," *Studio One*

Clockwise from top:
Loretta Young,
Perry Como,
Dragnet's Jack Webb,
Dinah Shore,
George Gobel

WHAT A YEAR IT WAS!

RADIO

FLASH!

THERE ARE AN ESTIMATED 8,200 RADIO STATIONS THROUGHOUT THE WORLD EITHER BROADCASTING OR BEING BUILT.

NATIONWIDE RADIO NETWORKS
NBC, ABC, CBS & Mutual Broadcasting

Top Network Radio Programs (Summer)

All-Star Football Game
Arthur Godfrey's
  Talent Scouts
Best Of Groucho
Dragnet
The FBI In Peace
  And War
The Gene Autry Show
The Jack Benny Show
Lux Radio Theatre
My Little Margie
Our Miss Brooks
People Are Funny
Treasury Agent
You Bet Your Life
Your Land And Mine

Other Radio Favorites

The Colgate Comedy Hour
Guiding Light
Helen Trent
House Party
Ma Perkins
The Martha Raye Show
The Milton Berle Show
My Little Margie
Our Gal Sunday
Perry Mason
Road of Life
This Is Nora Drake
Young Doctor Malone
Young Widder Brown

From left: Arthur Godfrey, Gene Autry

WHAT A YEAR IT WAS!

Signing Off
For The Last Time

Bobby Benson And The
 B-Bar-B Riders

The Hallmark
 Hall Of Fame

The Jack Benny Show
 (The Lucky Strike Program)

Just Plain Bill

The Lone Ranger

Lux Radio Theatre

Nick Carter,
 Master Detective

The Roy Rogers Show

Sergeant Preston
 Of The Yukon

Space Patrol

Stella Dallas

The University Of Chicago
 Round Table

The Whistler

Famous Birth
Fred Norris

ABC RADIO INTRODUCES "PERSONALIZED LISTENING" PROGRAMMING

ABC's new radio programming includes brief segments on subjects from marital counseling, family and career problems to inspirational messages and classical readings.

NBC's INNOVATIVE *MONITOR* PROGRAM DEBUTS

Broadcasting from locations around the world, NBC launches its innovative weekend *Monitor* series, the first 40-hour round-the-clock program featuring stories ranging from news and features to music, interviews and sports.

DON'T TOUCH THAT DIAL

According to a Nielsen poll, the greatest number of radio listeners prefer *Lux Radio Theatre* during the winter and *Dragnet* during the summer. *Ma Perkins* remains the daytime favorite throughout the year.

The Soviets permit CBS Radio correspondent **William Worthy** to begin broadcasting directly to the U.S.

NBC Radio launches its hour-long *Biographies in Sound*, re-creating the tragic life and happy times of **Zelda** and **F. Scott Fitzgerald**.

Milton Berle

F. Scott Fitzgerald

Motorola model 34F1

Here's a compact, lightweight portable phonograph that really travels in
high style. The handsome two-tone, airplane-luggage case is smartly finished
in rugged Green and White leatherette. The 3-speed phonograph plays
records of all sizes—all speeds—and plays them all as you've never
heard them before from a set priced as moderately as this. Two 5¼-inch
speakers project full-bodied sound to every corner of the room.
AC only. 18″ wide, 10½″ high, 15¼″ deep.

POPULAR

MUSIC

RECORDING STARS OF TOMORROW

Harry Belafonte

Chuck Berry

Pat Boone

The Dells

Etta James

Little Richard

Roger Williams

Chuck Berry

WE'RE HAVIN' A PARTY

More than 15,000 people purchase advance tickets for **Alan Freed's** first "Rock 'n' Roll Party" in New York City.

CHUCK BERRY ROCKS THE BLUES WITH A NEW SOUND

Chuck Berry's *Maybellene* hits #1 on *Billboard* and stays on the charts for 14 weeks.

A "TIMELY" HIT

Bill Haley's *Rock Around the Clock* hits #1 on the charts.

Etta James

The Penguins record *Earth Angel.*

1955

RCA demonstrates a music synthesizer.

MUSIC TO OUR EARS
Surveys conclusively prove that music in the workplace increases employee efficiency and productivity.

EMI MOVES INTO U.S. RECORD INDUSTRY
Electrical & Musical Industries, Inc. (EMI) buys control of Capitol Records (52%) and is moving into the U.S. market.

• PASSING •

Charlie "Bird" Parker, 34
A creative genius who joined his first band at age 14, saxophonist Parker was one of the musicians directly responsible for the development of bebop. When he moved to New York, he became close friends with Dizzy Gillespie, and often played with Gillespie, Miles Davis, Max Roach and Thelonious Monk. The famous jazz club Birdland was named after him, and he became known for his long, intricate improvisations.

Bird Lives!

Famous BIRTHS

Carlene **Carter**
Rosanne **Cash**
Steve **Earle**
Billy **Idol**
Yo-Yo **Ma**
Reba **McEntire**
Simon **Rattle**
Eddie **Van Halen**
Cassandra **Wilson**

HOT ALBUMS

Hoagy Carmichael's
Ol' Rockin' Chair

Tony Bennett's
Cloud 7

JAZZ COMBOS

Chet Baker
Dave Brubeck
John Lewis

Chet Baker

Gerry Mulligan
Shorty Rogers
Tony Scott

Gerry Mulligan

POPULAR BANDS

Ray Anthony
Count Basie
Les Brown
The Dorsey Brothers

Woody Herman

Les Elgart
Woody Herman
Stan Kenton
Billy May

BILLBOARD
POLL WINNERS TOP SINGERS
MALE **Frank Sinatra**
FEMALE **Doris Day**

Rosemary Clooney

COMPANION MAGAZINE'S LP OF THE MONTH
Rosemary Clooney's *While We're Young* LP is chosen hit of the month by WOMAN'S HOME COMPANION magazine and five famous disc jockeys.

KING COLE SINGS LOVE SONGS
Nat "King" Cole's "Darling, Je Vous Aime Beaucoup" and "The Sand and the Sea" are two of the beautiful ballads on WOMAN'S HOME COMPANION magazine's Record of the Month LP.

Dorothy Dandridge

Dorothy Dandridge sings at the Waldorf-Astoria's Empire Room while **Eartha Kitt** entertains her audience singing songs in English, French, Spanish and Turkish.

WHAT A YEAR IT WAS!

POPULAR SONGS

Ain't That A Shame

Pat Boone

Ain't That A Shame

Fats Domino

Autumn Leaves

Roger Williams

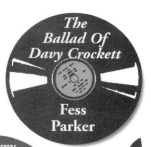

The Ballad Of Davy Crockett

Fess Parker

Black Denim Trousers

The Cheers

A Blossom Fell

Nat "King" Cole

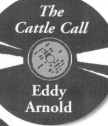

The Cattle Call

Eddy Arnold

Cherry Pink And Apple Blossom White

Perez Prado

Dance With Me Henry

Georgia Gibbs

Earth Angel

The Penguins

Earth Angel

The Crew-Cuts

Frank Sinatra

Nat "King" Cole

The Great Pretender

The Platters

Hard To Get

Gisele MacKenzie

He

Al Hibbler

Hearts Of Stone

The Fontane Sisters

I Don't Care

Webb Pierce

I Hear You Knocking

Gale Storm

In The Jailhouse Now

Webb Pierce

Learnin' The Blues

Frank Sinatra

Let Me Go, Lover

Joan Weber

Live Fast, Love Hard, Die Young
Faron Young

The Longest Walk
Jaye P. Morgan

Loose Talk
Carl Smith

Love And Marriage
Frank Sinatra

Love Is A Many-Splendored Thing
The Four Aces

Love Me Or Leave Me
Sammy Davis Jr.

Love, Love, Love
Webb Pierce

Mannish Boy
Muddy Waters

Memories Are Made Of This
Dean Martin

Moments To Remember
The Four Lads

Only You
The Hilltoppers

Only You
The Platters

A Satisfied Mind
Porter Wagoner

Bill Haley & His Comets

Seventeen
The Fontane Sisters

The Shifting Whispering Sands
Rusty Draper

Sincerely
The McGuire Sisters

Sixteen Tons
Tennessee Ernie Ford

Something's Gotta Give
The McGuire Sisters

That Do Make It Nice
Eddy Arnold

Tina Marie
Perry Como

Unchained Melody
Les Baxter

(We're Gonna) Rock Around The Clock
Bill Haley & His Comets

Whatever Lola Wants
Sarah Vaughan

The Yellow Rose Of Texas
Mitch Miller & His Orchestra

47-year-old **Herbert von Karajan** replaces the late **Wilhelm Furtwängler** as conductor of the Berlin Philharmonic.

PULITZER PRIZE WINNER—MUSIC

Gian-Carlo Menotti, *The Saint Of Bleecker Street*

38-year-old **Yehudi Menuhin** is recovering from a case of chicken pox, which he caught from his 6-year-old son, Gerard Yehudi Anthony Gould.

PREMIERES

Violin Concerto
ARTHUR BLISS

Sixth Symphony
DARIUS MILHAUD

Cantata of Psalms
ANTON HEILLER

Déserts
EDGAR VARÈSE

WALTER PISTON'S *Symphony No. 5* IS PRESENTED IN BOSTON.

THEY'RE ALL JUST STRINGING ALONG
50 female harpists ages 14-40 converge on Oberlin, Ohio for three days of playing under the direction of the most famous harpist of all, 70-year-old **Carlos Salzedo**.

WE'RE PACKING OUR VIOLINS AND HITTING THE ROAD
The New York Philharmonic and the Philadelphia Orchestra are off on European tours under the direction of **Dimitri Mitropoulos** and **Eugene Ormandy**, respectively.

A VERY SAD NOTE
Cellist **Pablo Casals** breaks his self-exile from Spain and returns to the town of El Vendrell to attend the funeral of his longtime friend and housekeeper, **Francisca Capdevila**.

Citing hostile cultural authorities, **Erich Kleiber** refuses to conduct in West Berlin.

The first international music festival is held in Athens, Greece.

With **Igor Stravinsky** conducting, the ninth annual Ojai Festival is held in Ojai, California.

Leopold Stokowski is invited to act as music director and conductor of Santa Barbara's Pacific Coast Music Festival.

Igor Stravinsky

WHAT A YEAR IT WAS!

Opera News —————— 1955

MARIAN ANDERSON DEBUTS AT THE MET

Marian Anderson, the first black to sing a major role at the Metropolitan Opera Company, is hailed by critics and audiences alike for her portrayal of the sorceress Ulrica in **Verdi's** *The Masked Ball*.

Tempestuous diva **Maria Meneghini Callas** hits a couple of really high C's as a U.S. marshal serves the Italian soprano with a summons following her farewell performance with the Lyric Theatre of Chicago.

Billy Daniels steps in after rotund tenor **Mario Lanza**, who shed 196 pounds for his $50,000-a-week engagement at Las Vegas' New Frontier Hotel, fails to perform due to laryngitis.

The Vienna State Opera opens a new hall to replace the one destroyed during World War II and presents **Beethoven's** *Fidelio*, which symbolizes the triumph of freedom.

Christel Goltz makes her Met debut in an unforgettable performance of the title role in **Strauss'** *Salome*, with debuting conductor **Dimitri Mitropoulos** magnificently conducting the orchestra.

OPERA PREMIERES

George Antheil's *The Wish* is presented by the Louisville Orchestra.

NBC Television Opera presents *Griffelkin* by **Lukas Foss**.

Werner Egk's opera *Irische Legende* premieres in Salzberg.

Sir William Walton's first opera, *Troilus and Cressida*, makes its American debut in San Francisco.

Sergei Prokofiev's opera *The Fiery Angel* opens in Venice.

Prokofiev's revised version of his opera *War and Peace* is performed for the first time in Leningrad.

Michael Tippett's *The Midsummer Marriage* opens in London.

From top: Marian Anderson, Maria Callas, Mario Lanza

Dance

The New York City Ballet breaks the record for successive nightly performances of one ballet after it dances *The Nutcracker* for seven straight weeks.

Margot Fonteyn is among the featured dancers as Sadler's Wells Ballet begins its fourth U.S. tour with a fall season at the Metropolitan Opera House, where it premieres the first American performances of its productions of *The Firebird, Les Sylphides, Scènes de Ballet, Rinaldo and Armida, The Lady and the Fool* and *Madame Chrysanthème*.

With music by **Giuseppe Verdi** and choreography by **Zachary Solov**, *Vittorio* is performed by the Metropolitan Opera Ballet.

The director of the Jacob's Pillow Dance Festival brings 10 members of the Royal Danish Ballet to America.

Doris Humphrey choreographs *Airs and Graces* at the American Dance Festival in New London, Connecticut and revives *The Shakers*, and **José Limón** premieres *Scherzo* and *Symphony for Strings*.

The U.S. State Department officially recognizes dance as an important part of its cultural exchange program and sponsors Ballet Theatre and José Limón in a South American tour as well as some of the European performances by the New York City Ballet.

A *Streetcar Named Desire* and *The Sphinx* are among the ballets added to the repertoire of Ballet Theatre for the 15th anniversary season at the Metropolitan Opera House.

KEEPING EVERYONE ON THEIR TOES

Capezio, Inc. makes a special grant to the dance department of New York City's High School for Performing Arts.

SHE MAY BE SMALL, BUT BOY DOES SHE PACK A PUNCH

Ballerina **Nora Kaye** dancing the role of Blanche DuBois in *A Streetcar Named Desire* accidentally jams her elbow into the eye of **Igor Youskevitch**, dancing Stanley Kowalski, knocking him out cold and later requiring eight stitches.

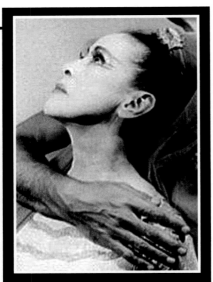

A season of modern dance at New York's ANTA Theater includes **Martha Graham's** *Ardent Song*, a revised version of *Theater for a Voyage*, and the José Limón Dance Company appearing in *The Traitor, Felipe el Loco* and other works.

Martha Graham receives the Henry Hadley medal for distinguished service to American music.

Three new dances become very popular: the cha-cha-cha, the merengue and the rock 'n' roll.

WHAT A YEAR IT WAS!

ON BROADWAY

Audiences in London attending Orson Welles' experiment in staging "Moby Dick" leave the theater feeling very confused as to the meaning of the production, but the London Times treats him with respect "and to an adventurer so valiant, our hearts go out, even when he comes to wreck."

ANOTHER OPENING, ANOTHER NIGHT

ALL IN ONE
☆
ALMOST CRAZY
☆
ANKLES AWEIGH
☆
BUS STOP
☆
CATCH A STAR
☆
CAT ON A HOT TIN ROOF
☆
CHAMPAGNE COMPLEX
☆
DAMN YANKEES

Kim Stanley in *Bus Stop*

WHAT A YEAR IT WAS!

Burl Ives and **Ben Gazzara** in *Cat on a Hot Tin Roof*

Barbara Bel Geddes in *Cat on a Hot Tin Roof*

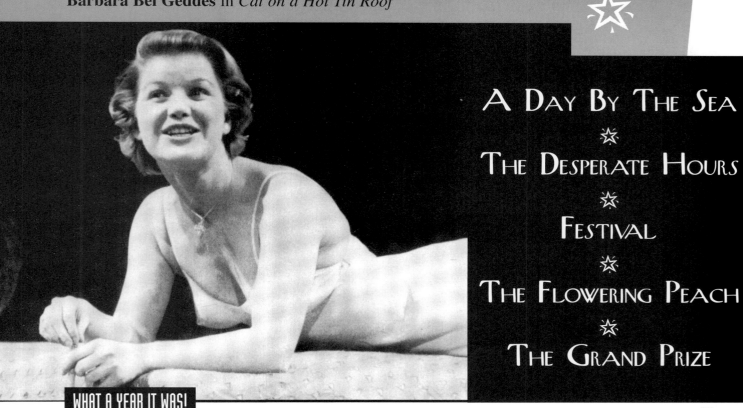

A Day By The Sea

☆

The Desperate Hours

☆

Festival

☆

The Flowering Peach

☆

The Grand Prize

WHAT A YEAR IT WAS!

1955

ANOTHER OPENING, ANOTHER NIGHT

A HATFUL
OF RAIN

✱

HEAR! HEAR!

✱

THE HONEYS

✱

HOUSE OF FLOWERS

✱

INHERIT THE WIND

✱

JANUS

✱

THE MATCHMAKER

✱

MAURICE CHEVALIER
IN AN EVENING
OF SONGS
AND IMPRESSIONS

Ed Begley and **Paul Muni**
in *Inherit the Wind*

ONCE UPON
A TAILOR

✱

PIPE DREAM

✱

PLAIN AND FANCY

✱

RED ROSES FOR ME

✱

SEVENTH HEAVEN

✱

SILK STOCKINGS

THE SOUTHWEST
CORNER

✱

THREE FOR
TONIGHT

✱

TONIGHT IN
SAMARKAND

✱

THE VAMP

✱

THE WAYWARD
SAINT

WHAT A YEAR IT WAS!

New York's Fulton Theatre is renamed in honor of the American theater's "grande dame," **Helen Hayes**, who is celebrating her 50th year on stage.

The American National Theatre and Academy (ANTA) has a smash hit with its revival of Thornton Wilder's Pulitzer Prize-winning play, *The Skin of Our Teeth*, starring **Helen Hayes** and **Mary Martin**.

Ballerina **Moira Shearer** makes the leap from ballet to stage starring in the touring company of *I Am a Camera*.

Robert Loggia is made a life member of New York's Actors Studio and stars in the Off-Broadway production of *The Man with the Golden Arm*.

On opening night, a London critic writes that despite the show being bland, **Danny Kaye** could "charm the ears off a turtle."

ON THE ROAD AGAIN

The U.S. government approves participation in the International Festival of Dramatic Arts in Paris and America is represented by *The Skin of Our Teeth* by **Thornton Wilder**, *Medea* starring **Judith Anderson**, and *Oklahoma!* starring **Shirley Jones** and **Jack Cassidy**.

The road company of *The Caine Mutiny Court-Martial* has its southern tour cut short following **Paul Douglas'** referral to the South as "a land of sowbelly and segregation."

"ODETS' FINEST PLAY!... WILL DELIGHT AND MOVE ANY THEATREGOER! SKULNIK GIVES A MEMORABLE PERFORMANCE! A MASTERPIECE OF ACTING!"
— BROOKS ATKINSON, *Times*

"SKULNIK IS IMMENSE! Casting him as Noah was sheer inspiration! Nothing I have seen all season is more memorable!" — RICHARD WATTS JR., *Post*

"SKULNIK IS IRRESISTIBLE! BERTA GERSTEN IS SUPERB! A genuine gayety, as warm as it is impudent, takes over the stage!"
— WALTER KERR, *Herald Tribune*

"THERE ARE HUNDREDS OF LAUGHS!"
— JOHN McCLAIN, *Jour-Amer.*

"FIRST-NIGHTERS GREETED IT WITH ROBUST LAUGHTER AND APPLAUSE!"
— ROBERT COLEMAN, *Mirror*

"SOMETHING HILARIOUS! Spontaneous, irresistible, warm, human comedy!"
— LOUIS SHEAFFER, *Eagle*

THE PRODUCERS THEATRE presents

MENASHA SKULNIK

THE FLOWERING PEACH

by CLIFFORD ODETS

"UPROARIOUS! Skulnik, with rich resources and comic timing, makes a memorable character of Noah. Berta Gersten is a dream!"
— WILLIAM HAWKINS, *World-Telegram*

FINAL CURTAIN

ANNIVERSARY WALTZ
THE BAD SEED
THE BOY FRIEND
THE CAINE MUTINY COURT~MARTIAL
CAN~CAN
DEAR CHARLES
THE DESPERATE HOURS
THE FLOWERING PEACH

KISMET
LUNATICS AND LOVERS
PETER PAN
THE RAINMAKER
THE SEVEN YEAR ITCH
THE SOLID GOLD CADILLAC
TEA AND SYMPATHY
THE TENDER TRAP

THE DEBUT OF **MACK THE KNIFE**

The Threepenny Opera, a modern version of **John Gay's** 18th-century *Beggar's Opera*, is staged at a Greenwich Village theater by **Kurt Weill** and **Bertolt Brecht**.

1955

TONY AWARDS

PLAY
THE DESPERATE HOURS

MUSICAL
THE PAJAMA GAME

DRAMATIC ACTOR
ALFRED LUNT
Quadrille

DRAMATIC ACTRESS
NANCY KELLY
The Bad Seed

MUSICAL ACTOR
WALTER SLEZAK
Fanny

MUSICAL ACTRESS
MARY MARTIN
Peter Pan

CHOREOGRAPHER
BOB FOSSE
The Pajama Game

COSTUME DESIGNER
CECIL BEATON
Quadrille

NEW YORK DRAMA CRITICS' CIRCLE AWARDS

BEST PLAY: Tennessee Williams
Cat On A Hot Tin Roof

BEST FOREIGN PLAY: Agatha Christie
Witness For The Prosecution

BEST MUSICAL: Gian-Carlo Menotti
The Saint Of Bleecker Street

Performing against a black backdrop, French panto-mimist Marcel Marceau dazzles a somewhat skeptical New York audience with the premiere of his brilliant one-man show, winning unanimous critical acclaim.

PULITZER PRIZE WINNER

Tennessee Williams' **Cat On A Hot Tin Roof** wins both the Pulitzer Prize and Drama Critics' Circle Award.

And Then They Wrote...

Anastasia (Guy Bolton) (adaptation)

A View From The Bridge (Arthur Miller)

Nekrassov (Jean-Paul Sartre)

The Balcony (Jean Genet)

The Man In The Gray Flannel Suit (Sloan Wilson)

WHAT A YEAR IT WAS!

The National Museum opens a remodeled area that includes gowns worn by America's first ladies in era-specific rooms.

OKAY, THOR, AND A 1-2-3
An exhibit on music at the San Diego Museum of Man includes a working jukebox that plays native tunes.

Washington, D.C. displays 100 drawings by **Francisco Goya**, treasures on loan from Spain.

PAINTING YOURSELF INTO A CORNER
El Greco's *Pieta* is on permanent loan to the Metropolitan Museum of Art from the **Stavros Niarchos** collection because the painting is too big for his house.

The Los Angeles County Museum assembles a comprehensive collection of **Renoir** paintings and sculptures.

70 works by the Dutch masters come to the U.S. courtesy of museums and private collectors in the Netherlands.

The Hague's Gemeentemuseum displays over 100 of **Piet Mondrian's** paintings.

Renoir's Le Chapeau Epingle

More than 500 photographs selected from 68 countries around the world are unveiled at **Edward Steichen's** *Family of Man* exhibit at the Museum of Modern Art in New York City. The acclaimed thematic exhibition presents a pictorial study of man from birth to death.

The Family of Man
Exhibition in New York

The **Whitney Museum** celebrates its 25th anniversary.

•

The **American Association of Museums** turns 50.

•

The **Pennsylvania Academy of Fine Arts** holds its 150th annual exhibit.

•

The **Eisenhower Museum** in Abilene, Kansas is dedicated.

Gemeentemuseum

WHAT A YEAR IT WAS!

Who says men don't understand women !

Whitman knows better!

Because it's the men who buy the Sampler more than anybody—at Christmastime and *all* the time.

And do you know what they do with all those boxes of chocolates? They give them away—to the ladies!

The gals all love this, of course. They like to be remembered (and like *you* for

remembering!). They like the candy too!

Whitman's chocolate is really something. It's an artful blend of three kinds of cocoa beans—the choicest varieties that come only from Ecuador, Trinidad and Venezuela.

How about the gals on *your* list? The Sampler is your answer, men. $2, $4, $6, $10.

New Pin Wheel package designed by Raymond Loewy, $1.50

CHOCOLATES

a gal never forgets the man who remembers

Stephen F. Whitman & Son, Inc., Philadelphia

98

Critics hail American contemporary artists **Willem de Kooning, Jackson Pollock, Robert Motherwell** and **Adolph Gottlieb** as more vital and original than their European counterparts—France's **Jean Dubuffet** and England's **Francis Bacon**.

New Works

Autobiography of Alice B. Shoe	**Andy Warhol**
Bed	**Robert Rauschenberg**
Don Quixote	**Pablo Picasso**
Target with Four Faces	**Jasper Johns**
The Lord's Supper	**Salvador Dali**
Yellow, Blue, Orange	**Mark Rothko**

Brancusi's The Kiss

21 works by **Willem de Kooning** are unveiled at the Martha Jackson Gallery.

Mark Rothko exhibits his paintings for the first time in four years at the Sidney Janis Gallery in New York.

French painter **Georges Mathieu**, reigning darling of advance-guard art, exhibits his "Lyrical Abstractionism" paintings at New York's Kootz Gallery.

Constantin Brancusi's exhibit of 59 works at the Guggenheim Museum in New York is hailed as a monument to asceticism.

Modern Art Museum features "The New Decade" in New York.

Over 5,000 visitors attend a **PABLO PICASSO** exhibit in one day at the Louvre in Paris. *Madame Z* and *The Women of Algiers,* as well as a portrait of Gertrude Stein from the turn of the century, are all included in the exhibit.

•

Paris celebrates Picasso's 75th birthday with a commemorative exhibition at the Musée des Arts Décoratifs.

•

Picasso teenage paintings discovered at his sister's home in Barcelona.

Picasso's Minotaur Caressing a Sleeping Woman, *1933*

1955

Rodin's sculpture honoring **Honoré de Balzac** is presented to the Museum of Modern Art.

Rodin's Balzac

The Frick Gallery acquires **Jan van Eyck's** famous *Rothschild Madonna*.

The Museum of Fine Arts in Boston acquires **Rembrandt's** *Twelfth Night*.

Rembrandt's *Portrait of a Young Man* is purchased for the Sumner Collection of the Wadsworth Atheneum in Hartford, Connecticut.

The Art Institute of Chicago acquires **Picasso's** *Woman and Child*. It also attains **Degas'** *Woman in a Rose Hat* and **Van Gogh's** *Self-Portrait*.

Roy Lichtenstein's *The Surrender of Weatherford to Jackson* is bought by the Butler Museum of American Art in Youngstown, Ohio.

New York's Metropolitan Museum acquires one of **Salvador Dali's** latest works for its permanent collection, a 6-foot surrealistic painting entitled *Crucifixion*.

Salvador Dali

A **Van Gogh** painting sells for $37,000.

In an auction of the Baron Cassel van Doorn art collection held at the Parke-Bernet Galleries in New York, two French 18th-century design Louis XV commodes are sold for $16,000. Also among the 416 pieces auctioned off are *St. John in the Wilderness* by **François Boucher** ($4,600) and a marble bust of the Marquis de Miromesnil, by 18th-century French sculptor **Jean-Antoine Houdon** ($6,000). The entire collection brings in $271,070.

PASSINGS

Fernand Léger, 74
Best known for his cubist paintings that often featured mechanical aspects and geometrical shapes, Léger also incorporated elements of architecture, fauvism, surrealism and neoclassicism into his works.

Yves Tanguy, 55
Greatly influenced by André Breton, and one of the original members of the surrealist school in Paris, Tanguy had his first solo exhibit in 1927 at the Galerie Surréaliste in Paris.

Maurice Utrillo, 71
Utrillo was influenced by Impressionism and often painted the local scenes of the Montmartre quarter of Paris, where he was born. With the encouragement of his artist mother, after a bout with alcoholism and a stay in a sanitarium, Utrillo began to paint. He was awarded the Cross of the Legion of Honor by the French government, and several years later painted one of his most famous paintings, *Montmartre Street Corner/ Lapin Agile*.

Yves Tanguy drawing

WHAT A YEAR IT WAS!

Books

Charles Dickens

According to some of France's top thinkers, *Great Expectations* by **Charles Dickens** and *War and Peace* by **Leo Tolstoy** are the two best fiction works written by non-French writers between 1850 and 1950.

Approximately 300 million paperbacks are sold in the U.S.

The NEW YORKER celebrates its 30th anniversary.

Recordings of poets and authors reading their works become increasingly available and popular. Some top choices include **Dylan Thomas, T.S. Eliot, Colette, Edith Sitwell** and **James Joyce**.

The *Journal of Major George Washington*, printed in 1754, sells for $25,000.

Carl Sandburg refuses to state his feelings about a certain poem, saying, "I've never been a judge in a poetry contest... My wife has judged a lot of goats in contests."

Walt Whitman's *Leaves of Grass* celebrates its 100th anniversary.

BETTER LATE THAN NEVER

Originally released in 1940, **Ernest Hemingway's** For Whom the Bell Tolls *is finally reviewed in the Soviet Union.* "A talented book," *the magazine* News *declares, though* "somehow it failed to say what we had been hoping to hear. . . ."

A REVOLUTION IN THE MAKING

At Six Gallery in San Francisco, **Allen Ginsberg** reads Howl *for the first time. In attendance are* **Michael McClure, Gary Snyder, Kenneth Rexroth** and **Jack Kerouac**. *Kerouac cheers Ginsberg along with shouts of* "Go!"

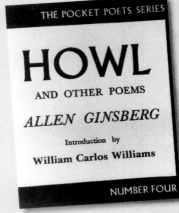

THE POCKET POETS SERIES

HOWL

AND OTHER POEMS

ALLEN GINSBERG

Introduction by

William Carlos Williams

NUMBER FOUR

POETS REVISITED

Two of America's greatest poets, **Walt Whitman** and **Emily Dickinson**, are honored through major publications chronicling their lives and works.

Walt Whitman

Nearly 100 bookmobiles travel around rural Kentucky, giving the 40% of the state's residents without libraries an opportunity to borrow books.

Mrs. Charlemae Rollins, children's librarian at the Chicago Public Library, wins a $500 Grolier Foundation Award because she "has led thousands of children to read good books."

The Association of School Librarians battles against censorship with its "School Library Bill of Rights."

Work begins on the Truman Presidential Museum and Library in Independence, Missouri.

1955 Books

Andersonville
MacKinlay Kantor

•

Auntie Mame
Patrick Dennis

•

Band Of Angels
Robert Penn Warren

•

Bell's Landing
Gerald Warner Brace

•

Bonjour Tristesse
Françoise Sagan

•

**The Bride Of The
Innisfallen**
Eudora Welty

•

The Dark Arena
Mario Puzo

•

The Deer Park
Norman Mailer

•

Eloise
Kay Thompson

**Gift From
The Sea**
Anne Morrow
Lindbergh

•

**The Genius
And The
Goddess**
Aldous Huxley

•

**A Good Man Is
Hard To Find**
Flannery O'Connor

•

**The Good
Shepherd**
C.S. Forester

•

High Adventure
Sir Edmund Hillary

•

Inside Africa
John Gunther

•

Journey To Love
William Carlos
Williams

•

Lolita
Vladimir Nabokov

*Aldous
Huxley*

**Love, Death
And The
Ladies' Drill Team**
Jessamyn West

•

Love Poems
Gloria Vanderbilt

•

**The Man
In The
Gray Flannel Suit**
Sloan Wilson

•

**Marjorie
Morningstar**
Herman Wouk

•

The Mint
T.E. Lawrence

•

Moonraker
Ian Fleming

•

Mother And Son
Ivy Compton-Burnett

James Baldwin

**The Mouse
That Roared**
Leonard Wibberley

•

**Notes Of A
Native Son**
James Baldwin

•

**Officers And
Gentlemen**
Evelyn Waugh

•

**Pictures Of The
Gone World**
Lawrence Ferlinghetti

•

Predilections
Marianne Moore

•

**A Prospect
Of The Sea**
Dylan Thomas
(posthumously)

**The Quiet
American**
Graham Greene

•

A Rose For Winter
Laurie Lee

•

The Sane Society
Erich Fromm

•

**The Scrolls From
The Dead Sea**
Edmund Wilson

•

**The Shield
Of Achilles**
W.H. Auden

•

**Sincerely,
Willis Wayde**
John P. Marquand

•

**Something Of
Value**
Robert Ruark

•

**Surprised By Joy:
The Shape Of My
Early Life**
C.S. Lewis

**The Talented
Mr. Ripley**
Patricia Highsmith

•

**Ten
North Frederick**
John O'Hara

•

**A Train
Of Powder**
Rebecca West

•

**The Vestal Lady
On Brattle
And
Other Poems**
Gregory Corso

•

Waterfront
Budd Schulberg

•

**Why Johnny
Can't Read**
Rudolf Flesch

•

Year Of Decisions
Harry S. Truman

Mystery Writers of America Award

Best Mystery Novel
Raymond Chandler,
The Long Goodbye

Shelby Foote
is awarded a
Guggenheim Fellowship.

National Book Awards

Fiction	**William Faulkner**, *A Fable*
Nonfiction	**Joseph W. Krutch**, *The Measure of Man*
Poetry	**Wallace Stevens**, Collected Poems
Special Citation	**e. e. cummings**, Poems: 1923-1954

Hey There, Sonny

Jean Cocteau is elected to the French Academy. With the average age of its 40 members hovering around 77, Cocteau, at age 63, is by far the baby of the bunch.

American Academy of Arts & Letters

Jack Kerouac receives a grant.

Howells Medal for American Fiction

Eudora Welty,
The Ponder Heart
The award is given every five years "for the most distinguished work of American fiction published during that period."

Jack Kerouac

FamousBirth
John Grisham

Passings

Thomas Mann, 80
World-renowned German author Mann received the Nobel Prize for Literature in 1929. He immigrated to the United States in 1938 and is best known for *Buddenbrooks, Death in Venice* and *The Magic Mountain*. During World War II, Mann broadcast anti-Nazi sentiments for Germans.

NOBEL PRIZE WINNER

LITERATURE
Halldór K. Laxness,
Iceland

PULITZER PRIZE WINNERS

- BIOGRAPHY
  William S. White,
  The Taft Story
- HISTORY
  Paul Horgan,
  Great River: The Rio Grande in North American History
- FICTION
  William Faulkner,
  A Fable
- AMERICAN POETRY
  Wallace Stevens,
  Collected Poems

Wallace Stevens, 75

Poet and businessman Stevens once said of poetry, "It's the way of making one's experience, almost wholly inexplicable, acceptable."
Stevens, an insurance company vice president, was awarded the Pulitzer Prize for Poetry, the Bollingen Prize in Poetry and the Gold Medal of the Poetry Society of America.

WHAT A YEAR IT WAS!

FASHION  1955

THE "AMERICAN WOMAN" LOOK

The summer of 1955 brings us gay, casual clothing ranging from Orlon® sweaters to silk and denim dresses, terry cloth shirts and shorts in a multitude of fabrics from calf-skin to velvet. The popularity of toreador pants grows, and cotton knits are the craze. Other favorite fabrics include rayon taffeta, rayon crepe and satin trim.

FASHION DESIGNER CLAIRE McCARDELL

CLAIRE McCARDELL,

the designer who gave the American woman a look of her own, introduces her summer collection ranging from $10 to $50 for play clothes, $29 to $100 for dresses and $89 to $150 for suits and coats.

WHAT A YEAR IT WAS!

the latest in fur

Top California society turns out to see the latest in fur at a charity to aid handicapped children.

Model wears chinchilla coat valued at $100,000.

Iris mink has price tag of $10,000.

bonnets from

The latest millinery fashions from Italy reveal a trend toward wide brims of lightweight fur utilizing ostrich feathers and netting.

OSTRICH FEATHERS
ingeniously accent this cute little chapeau.

sunny italy

A LITTLE TURBAN suitable for a rajah's favorite.

A RUSSIAN CAP, old-fashioned and old-worldish.

THE NET
goes all out this time, but the eyes have it.

1955

evening gowns from Paris

Paris designers reveal their latest creations.

Elegant dinner-to-theater ensemble in Orlon satin emphasizes unbelted line.

This black cocktail dress by Jacques Heim tapers from snug bodice to wide hem.

Christian Dior creates an adaptation of the "midi" in this dinner gown with buttons down the back.

A French tapestry inspired this short evening gown by Pierre Balmain with exquisite three-dimensional embroidery.

The embroidery marks this as a Balmain creation with its intricate shirring and sculpted bodice emphasizing the supple drape of the fabric—rich white satin of man-made fibers.

Seated:
Marc Bohan's elegant ball gown from Paris: a first look at a new style from France soon to adorn the American woman.

Standing:
Jacques Heim's "telescope" silhouette.

Summer-sky lawn, trailing star sapphire buttons down the lean torso. By Jerry Gilden. About $13, at leading stores.

Not a shadow of a doubt with Kotex

You're the picture of confidence — for Kotex sanitary napkins give you the complete absorbency you need . . . the softness you're sure of. Kotex holds its shape, keeps its comfortable fit. No roping, twisting or chafing. Moreover, you can't make a mistake because this napkin can be worn on either side, safely. And Kotex is the only leading brand with special, flat pressed ends that prevent revealing outlines.

New soft grey package. Your choice of Regular Kotex — blue panel; Junior — green panel; Super — rose panel.

MORE WOMEN CHOOSE KOTEX* THAN ALL OTHER SANITARY NAPKINS

Know someone who needs to know? Remember how puzzled *you* were when "that" day arrived for the first time? Maybe you know some youngster *now* who's in the same boat. Help her out! Send today for the new *free booklet* "You're A Young Lady Now." Written for girls 9 to 12, it tells her all she needs to know, *beforehand*. Button-bright! Write P.O. Box 3434, Dept. 255, Chicago 11, Ill.

*T.M. REG. U.S. PAT. OFF.

112

NO elbow ROOM

Christian Dior declares elbows the least attractive part of a woman's body.

36-24-36

After nine years of taking measurements, the Department of Commerce has come up with a uniform sizing system for women that will stay the same for all clothing and all designers.

The permanent wave marks its 50th anniversary.

it's a dog's life— a $500 million industry

With dog owners ever searching for the latest in doggie apparel, most department stores now carry fashionable designer accessories ranging from cocktail hats, mink collar coats, sequin and ermine collars to earrings, maternity coats, weight reduction machines and the ever-popular scent, Kennel #9 (1 oz. $3).

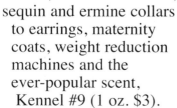

WHAT A YEAR IT WAS!

THE ENSEMBLE OUTFIT
Matching coat and dress or two-piece suit with a matching wool or satin overblouse

The long, clingy **EVENING DRESS**

TWEED SUITS

Christian Dior's **A-LINE** collection

THE SHEATH is the most popular dress style.

POODLE SKIRTS worn with saddle shoes and bobby sox are all the rage with girls.

WHAT ABOUT GRAY?

Researchers at Johns Hopkins University have discovered women's feet look bigger in white shoes than they do in black shoes.

The New York City Transit Authority has deemed women's fashions to be safety hazards. Contributing to injuries sustained while on buses are sling pumps, slim skirts and slippery materials, the latter sometimes causing women to slip right out of their seats.

A warning to all earring-loving women: heavy earrings with spring backs may cause earlobes to tear.

Record-size 120 carat diamond is cut down to 60 carats after 2 months of work.

designer **MARY QUANT** opens shop in London.

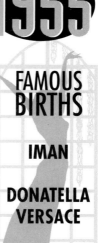

FAMOUS BIRTHS

IMAN

DONATELLA VERSACE

ADMIRED FASHIONABLE WOMEN

MARLENE **DIETRICH**

HELEN **HAYES**

MME. CHIANG **KAI-SHEK**

HELEN **KELLER**

PATRICIA "PAT" **NIXON**

QUEEN SORAYA **OF IRAN**

DUCHESS OF **WINDSOR**

Marlene Dietrich

DACRON, a tricot knit no-iron fabric, hits the market.

all that glitters...a bargain Tiffany style

Tiffany's New York throws its first bargain sale, attracting 2,400 customers in one day who snatch up bargain merchandise ranging from a silver tea set reduced from $12,500 to $6,000 to a ladies' compact reduced from $2,375 to $1,500. Still available is a stone from a sultan's belt buckle reduced to only $29,000 from the original asking price of $36,300.

WHAT A YEAR IT WAS!

american man look

THE AMERICAN MALE

finally becomes a peacock as the new emphasis on color and casualness livens up drab wardrobes. Yellows, reds, tartan stripes and attractive checks are now found on clothing ranging from shorts to jackets.

New York's **BROOKS BROTHERS** sells casual checked and striped clothes for evening.

President Eisenhower wears a blue straw hat during the summer.

California designers bring out shorter slacks and pleated sports jackets.

THE MOTORCYCLE LOOK

is one of the rages with young men as they dress in the image of movie idol Marlon Brando, while others choose the James Dean look, which includes Levi's blue jeans and a pack of cigarettes rolled up in the arm of a white T-shirt.

The West grew up in Levi's

PATRONIZE YOUR HOMETOWN MERCHANT – HE'S YOUR NEIGHBOR

LEVI'S®
AMERICA'S FINEST® OVERALL
SINCE 1850

1955 ADVERTISEMENT

Davy Crockett fad sweeps the U.S.

Walt Disney launches a national Davy Crockett craze with his television series shot in color starring Fess Parker.

Davy Crockett merchandise ranging from coonskin caps and leather jackets to balloons and bicycles rings up sales to the tune of $100,000,000 by midyear, with sales projections of double that amount by year-end.

With the retail market being fickle, however, by September the fad begins to fade and many warehouses are left overflowing with unsold coonskin caps.

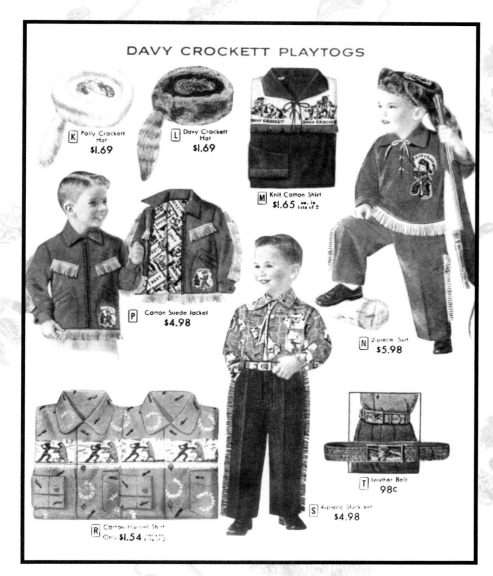

DAVY CROCKETT PLAYTOGS

K Polly Crockett Hat $1.69

L Davy Crockett Hat $1.69

M Knit Cotton Shirt $1.65 ea. in lots of 2

P Cotton Suede Jacket $4.98

N 2-piece Suit $5.98

T Leather Belt 98c

S 4-piece Slack set $4.98

R Cotton Flannel Shirt Only $1.54

THE *FORWARD* LOOK

"7 top fashion designers find Chrysler Corporation's 1955 cars a stimulating new concept of good design."

L. L. Colbert, President

Left to right: Tom Brigance • Anne Fogarty • Clare Potter • Lily Daché • Nettie Rosenstein • Pauline Trigere • Claire McCardell

At a special advance showing in New York, the celebrated fashion designers, above, saw a line of motor cars that was bright and alive and *wholly new*. And what they saw, you can see soon!

They saw Chrysler Corporation's new 1955 cars—Plymouth, Dodge, De Soto, Chrysler, Imperial—the cars with the all-new concept of style we call THE FORWARD LOOK.

These experts found THE FORWARD LOOK a design that matches the moods, needs and attitudes of today's motor car owners . . . and does it in a fresh and imaginative way.

They admired the all-new contemporary design, the *long, low lines* that America's motorists have been eager for. They were struck by the *look of motion* these cars give even when they are standing still.

The beauty and astonishing visibility offered by the New-Horizon windshields delighted them—for these are the only fully swept-back, fully wrapped-around windshields on any car.

They were attracted to the *rich fabrics* and the compelling new *colors*. They found wonderful convenience in the unique new position of the PowerFlite Range Selector.

THE FORWARD LOOK that intrigued these famous designers will no doubt intrigue you, too. We believe you will find in these cars just what you've wanted, just what you've asked for and hoped for in your next motor car. In a few days, you'll be able to see THE FORWARD LOOK. Don't miss it!

On Display November 17! The 1955 PLYMOUTH • DODGE • DE SOTO • CHRYSLER • IMPERIAL

CHRYSLER CORPORATION ⟩ THE *FORWARD* LOOK

COPYRIGHT 1954 CHRYSLER CORPORATION

See Chrysler Corporation's great new full-hour TV Shows—"Shower of Stars" every 4th Thursday . . . "Climax!" the 3 intervening Thursdays. CBS-TV, 8:30-9:30 P.M., EST.

New PRODUCTS & INVENTIONS

V ideo telephone of tomorrow unveiled at the Western Electronics convention in San Francisco.

Cost: $5,000 per phone.

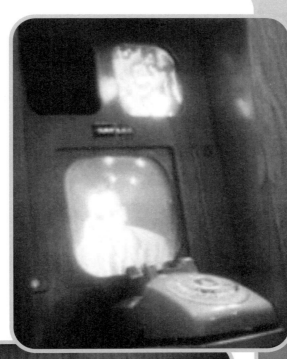

HELLO, OPERATOR

The United States has approximately 56,000,000 telephones while there are approximately 101,000,000 worldwide.

CAN HAL BE FAR AWAY?

IBM begins the development of the model 704, the first computer with a programming language.

Bell Telephone develops transistorized components, reducing the size of a large-capacity computer from room size to 3 cubic feet.

1955

SPECIAL K

is the newest cereal from Kellogg.

Betty Crocker Crustquick PIE CRUST MIX

General Mills announces that **Betty Crocker** is getting a face-lift to make her look more like a sincere housewife. Marketing surveys revealed Betty looked too much like a career girl.

THERE COULD BE A NEW CAN IN YOUR FUTURE

Coca-Cola begins testing canned Cokes, shipping 100,000 cartons to the Army and Air Force Exchange Service in the Far East. If successful, they will try the idea on civilian markets.

Coca-Cola changes bottle size from 6 ounces to 10 ounces and introduces 12- and 26-ounce king-size and family-size bottles.

COULD BE A BITTER PILL TO SWALLOW

Encouraged by the success of its fresh orange juice, a Florida company is testing the sale of fresh, unsweetened grapefruit juice for 30¢ a quart in New York and, if successful, will go national.

ADD SOME COLD WATER AND PRESTO

Soon to hit your grocer's freezer case is frozen concentrated orange and grapefruit juice.

Owens-Illinois Glass expands its application of an airtight container cap that hermetically reseals a glass jar developed for baby food packers to a variety of sizes for food and drug items.

IF YOU DON'T MIND, I'LL PASS ON THIS ONE

Licorice-, root beer- and lime-flavored milk is about to be test-marketed in Detroit under the brand name "Moo Gay" and will sell for 10¢ a can.

INSTANT MOO JUICE

With the development of a splash-proof pump, vending machines dispensing milk into paper cups may be coming to theaters or office buildings sometime in the near future.

INSTANT *Hot & Cold* COFFEE BREAK

With the introduction of a new office drinking fountain with hot and cold faucets, the coffee break takes on a new social dimension as employees are now able to brew their own refreshments instantly.

WHAT A YEAR IT WAS!

is introduced.

 RCA demonstrates a music synthesizer.

WITH FLYING COLORS
Fred Morrison creates a plastic flying disc and sells it to **WHAM-O**.

Your kids can now listen to their favorite television program without bothering you, thanks to a new headset device that attaches to the audio system of your television set.

Philco Corp. develops a 7 1/2-pound portable phonograph that uses transistors instead of vacuum tubes.

Raytheon introduces a portable radio that will play for 2,500 hours without a battery change.

A BREATH OF FRESHER AIR
Raytheon Manufacturing claims that their new "Micronnaire" can remove more than 99% of all smoke, dust, pollen and even some types of bacteria from room air.

OPEN SESAME
A new device is being offered that will open your garage door or gate by remote control.

Aluminum and plastics are new materials heavily utilized by the construction industry.

Floor tiles, skylights and acrylic domes show signs of coming into standard use.

GETTING INTO THE SWIM OF THINGS
An oval glass-fiber swimming pool selling for around $2,500 is being marketed by a Los Angeles company.

SCRUB NO MORE
A new silicone-coating process will now make it easier to get rid of caked-on food from pots and pans.

Philco buys the patent rights to a pullout griddle plate built into an oven and **Proctor Electric** does the same for a new, completely automatic pressure cooker.

BUILT-IN KITCHENS—STANDARD EQUIPMENT OF THE FUTURE
Celebrating its 50th anniversary, Hotpoint introduces a new range with quick-heating burners and announces that market studies indicate custom kitchens could become standard equipment in 20 to 30 years.

● Kodak debuts fast 35mm Ektachrome film.

NEW PRODUCTS

Vibrating toothbrush

Crest is introduced, the first toothpaste to use fluoride.

Singing teakettle with electric plug

Wall-mounted refrigerator/freezer

REMINGTON RAND
UNIVAC

Not on the Drawing Board, Not "On Order"...
IN ACTUAL BUSINESS USE!

The Remington Rand Univac is the *only* completely self-checked electronic data-processing system now being delivered ...the only one actually proven in business use. No comparable system handles alphabetic and numeric data to turn out payrolls, control inventories, and perform the other down-to-earth routine tasks vital to American industry.

In today's competitive market, the company which cuts its overhead *first* comes out on top. Univac is already at work in many organizations, so don't wait until 1956...1957...or 1958 to cash in on the tremendous savings available with this large-scale electronic business system. The time to act is *now*, to prevent your lagging perilously behind competition in the years to come.

There's no need to wait for equipment which is "just around the corner." Read why, in an impartial article on electronic computing for business, written by management consultants of a nationally known public accounting firm. Write to Room 1267, at the address below, for your free copy of this informative survey, "Electronics Down To Earth."

Remington Rand
Electronic Computing Department • 315 Fourth Avenue • New York 10

120

Amphibious motorcycle is invented by Antonio Carma in Spain.

World's largest crochet hook is invented in Nuremberg, Germany.

A patent is issued for an atomic clock, accurate to one second in 100,000 years based on the constant, natural vibration frequency of atoms in ammonia or other molecules.

U.S. **Rubber Co.** brings out a special golf ball for women named the "U.S. Queen Royal" in which the rubber strips are wound less tightly.

A new field ion microscope developed by physicist **Erwin Mueller** offers a clearer image of all atoms on the surface of a specimen.

DOES IT SAY "GOD BLESS YOU" IF YOU SNEEZE?

Westinghouse installs its first "phantom voice" on an elevator in a New York office building, which calls out messages such as "This car up," "Going down," or "Press your floor button."

SHEDDING LIGHT IN THOSE DARK CORNERS

General Electric comes out with a new and more efficient miniature lamp to be used in appliances.

The new "nightlighter" automatically turns your lights on and off according to whether it's light or dark outside.

700,000,000 LIRA EQUALS WHAT?

Figuring out foreign currency conversion is now made simple with this new "Instant Calculator," which easily fits into your passport.

TO LOOK SHARP

A safety razor with backup refills and used blade disposal is invented by **Joseph Muros** and **Louis V. Nigro**, who assign the patent to the **Gillette Company**.

Scripto beats **Parker Pen Company** to the marketplace introducing a new liquid graphite pencil that looks like a lead pencil but writes like a ballpoint pen.

GETTING A STAMP OF APPROVAL

A new rubber stamp containing its own ink supply is introduced by a Brooklyn company and will retail for $1.00 or $2.00 for a custom stamp such as "Paid," "Special Delivery" or "Fragile."

A Minneapolis company is marketing white ink for use in industrial marking that dries fast and will not flake or rub off.

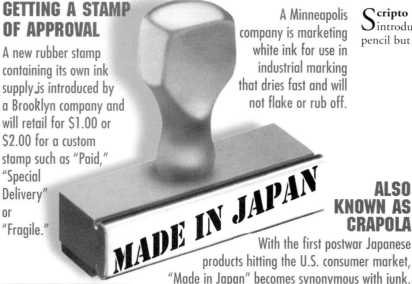

ALSO KNOWN AS CRAPOLA

With the first postwar Japanese products hitting the U.S. consumer market, "Made in Japan" becomes synonymous with junk.

General Electric scientists create industrial diamonds.

WHAT A YEAR IT WAS!

AMERICA TAKES TO THE ROAD... IN CARS THAT ARE BIGGER, MORE POWERFUL AND MORE COLORFUL

Americans anxious to buy high-performance cars are finding showrooms filled with gleaming new models in such fashionable colors as **peach**, **sea green**, **coral**, **yellow** and the nation's current favorite—**pink**.

Automobile manufacturers have added extra horsepower and inches to their 1955 models, along with attractive seatcover fabrics, wraparound windshields and ultra-modern streamlined styling.

WOMAN DESIGNS SCUFFPROOF TIRE

Maria Gottschall, the only woman in the field of tire development, designs a white sidewall scuffproof tire. The band of black solves the problem of curb marks on the white tire.

"Idea" cars embodying the latest in automotive styling are previewed in New York.

These futuristic cars will not go into production but will guide engineers of America's major companies that spend millions on the development of these models, paving the way for equally remarkable advances in future production models.

This sleek, two-passenger car represents American sports car styling. An externally mounted exhaust system attests to the power of this low-slung dream buggy.

WAIT FOR THAT BUZZER

A traffic signal for blind pedestrians has been installed in Louisville, Kentucky.

Harley-Davidson Motor Co. brings out the "Hummer," a new lightweight motorcycle selling for around $320 that will get up to 100 miles per gallon.

YOU MIGHT GET A CHARGE OUT OF THIS ONE

A Los Angeles company invents the first practical turbo supercharger for heavy-duty tractors and earthmovers.

GM introduces a 15-inch sun-powered car model.

Remote Control for TV

Fig. 1. The Emerson model 1158 remote-control unit shown here is capable of duplicating all of the TV set's front panel adjustments for picture and sound.

In many cases these units are furnished with the set, but, they can be installed by any service technician.

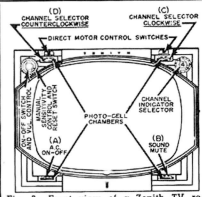

Fig. 2. Front view of a Zenith TV receiver with the "Flash-Matic" remote control, showing the various components.

E.I. DuPont de Nemours & Co. announces that it has successfully produced paper from synthetic fibers which is 3 to 10 times stronger than that made of rags or pulp and has 200 times the resistance to folding.

E.I. DuPont develops a no-iron Dacron called "Fantastique"—a tricot knit fabric made of polyester yarn that is easily laundered, fast-drying, wrinkle-resistant and requires no ironing.

IT'S NOW SAFE TO STEP IN THOSE PUDDLES

A silicone product that waterproofs leather has been developed by the Dow Corning Corp. and will be tested on a new combination work and sports boot.

Quick-acting parachute developed in England.

The first self-service ticket vending machine is introduced in Manhattan's Grand Central Station.

The first stair-climbing, electrically driven wheelchair is invented in Denmark.

TWINKLE, TWINKLE, LITTLE EARS
Electric earrings that blink on and off as the wearer walks are being marketed by a company out of Fairfield, New Jersey.

A new unbreakable eyeglass lens is developed in Great Britain.

Combination hearing aid and glasses hit the market in New York.

PASSINGS

George Ball, 82
Along with his brothers, philanthropist Ball began Ball Brothers, producers of Mason fruit jars.

Hubert C. Booth, 83
Inventor of the first vacuum cleaner.

Glenn Martin, 69
Martin was one of America's pioneering pilots and received one of the first pilot's licenses in the U.S. His company manufactured planes, jet fighters and satellites for the government and private companies.

WHAT A YEAR IT WAS!

SCIENCE

& MEDICINE

The B-52, America's biggest and newest jet bomber, goes into squadron service with the Strategic Air Command at Castle Air Force Base in California.

The mightiest bomber in history threatens devastation to America's enemies.

The Army unveils still another radical step forward in its aerial armada— the "convertiplane."

Making its first test flights in Texas, the convertiplane combines the best features of the helicopter, with the ability to rise vertically, and the speed of conventional aircraft.

The three-bladed rotors are mounted on the ends of the 30-foot wings. When sufficient altitude is attained, the rotors can be tilted forward in about 10 seconds. The plane is expected to attain a speed of 175 mph.

atomic ENERGY

The U.S. Atomic Energy Commission releases a report disclosing that 7,000 square miles were contaminated with lethal radioactive fallout as a result of the H-bomb detonated in the Pacific in March 1954.

U.S. agrees to pay $2,000,000 for damages to Japanese fishermen resulting from an H-bomb explosion in 1954.

Atomic testing series in Nevada by U.S. Atomic Commission results in 14 explosions.

A model of a typical American community holds up well in a nuclear blast test conducted in the Nevada desert.

2,000 Marines, 3,500 yards from a Las Vegas test site, are dusted with atomic fallout.

The Atomic Energy Commission announces that nuclear power plants will soon be open to private ownership.

Two new nuclear particles are identified in Rochester, New York, bringing the total to 21.

HOPING FOR A NON-EXPLOSIVE ENDING

New York's Con Ed to build the first private nuclear power plant at Indian Point.

The Atomic Energy Commission approves plans for private nuclear reactors in the Chicago and Detroit areas.

72 nations attend the first International Conference on the Peaceful Uses of Energy in Geneva, with the United States leading the world in urging shifting of focus from military to peaceful use of atomic energy. Britain and the U.S. sign joint cooperation agreements to use atomic energy for both peacetime and defense purposes.

✷ Discovery of anti-proton atomic particle announced at University of California.

At Sea

The navy unveils a new look in submarines with the testing of the Albacore (above)—which embodies many radical changes in hull design.

Built to spend most of its time submerged, the sub is shorter and rounder than previous undersea craft and will provide the Navy data on which future atomic vessels will be planned.

A BIGGER BANG FOR THE BUCK

The AEC announces its ability to build an H-bomb of virtually limitless size.

GREAT BRITAIN announces ability to make H-bombs.

FIRST MISSILE with atomic warhead tested.

THE U.S. ARMY stages a mock atomic raid for visiting Soviets.

U.S.S.R. EXPLODES its most powerful nuclear bomb.

The *Nautilus*, the world's first atomic-powered submarine, is launched. A sister ship, the *Sea Wolf*, is launched later in the year.

WHAT A YEAR IT WAS!

Photosynthesis, the conversion of solar energy into fuel by green plants, is traced by California scientists.

South African cave discoveries reveal the earliest evidence of man's first use of tools and fire.

THAT'S ONE BIG ROCK

Weighing 103 pounds, the largest specimen of super-grade uranium ore ever mined is on display in the Morgan Hall of Minerals and Gems at New York's American Museum of Natural History.

WHY, YOU OLD FOSSIL, YOU

Columbia University oceanographers announce the discovery on the floor of the Atlantic Ocean muddy sediments containing fossil sea animals estimated to be at least 100 million years old.

Plans for launching an artificial orbiting satellite into space by 1957 or 1958 are announced by the National Academy of Sciences and the National Science Foundation. The U.S.S.R. announces its plans to build and launch its own satellite in the International Geophysical Year 1957-1958.

✴ The U.S.S.R. establishes a permanent commission for interplanetary communications.

✴ The National Geographic Society announces the discovery of a large blue-green area on the planet Mars which was thought to be vegetation.

✴ 100 German scientists work for U.S. in development of guided missiles.

✴ An armed Nike guided missile escapes the launching pad and explodes in flight.

Nike missile

THE ANSWER, DEAR BRUTUS, IS IN THE ROCKS

Tests conducted on two samples of meteorites by scientists at the University of Chicago indicate that they were formed almost five billion years ago.

IT'S IN THE STARS

The longest solar eclipse since A.D. 717 takes place on June 19th and 20th.

strike!

Carrier Task Force
Helps Defend America's Freedom

Strike!...a carrier strike against enemy forces is one of our most spontaneous and devastating weapons ...a potent force for peace in a troubled world.

Strike!...carrier task forces, teamed with long range, land-based Air Power, patrol the seas ready to deliver shattering destruction when and where needed.

Strike!...your New Air Navy is jet propelled. Aircraft like the Chance Vought F7U-3 *Cutlass* arm mobile carrier forces with terrific power. Power that helps carry out your Navy's vital mission: control of the seas that cover 70% of the world.

Navy Fliers Challenge the Jet Frontier
Action, adventure...fellowship...prestige... and priceless training that fits you for the challenge of the new jet age...all wait for you as a Navy flier. If you are 18-25 and single, visit your nearest Naval Air Station or write NAVCAD, Washington 25, D.C.

CHANCE VOUGHT AIRCRAFT
INCORPORATED · DALLAS, TEXAS

SUNNY DAYS AHEAD?
For the first time, Bell Telephone uses solar energy to power a phone call.

SCORE ONE FOR SUNSHINE
Talks on the use of solar power open in Tucson, Arizona.

MIT produces high-frequency waves.

I SEE A RING IN HIS WIFE'S FUTURE
A General Electric scientist has invented a process for creating garnets, a dark red gemstone.

IT'S THERE BECAUSE WE SAY IT'S THERE
The University of California reports the discovery of Element 101, a synthetic unit of matter that does not exist in nature and has never before been observed on earth.

WHAT'S A FEW MILLION YEARS BETWEEN FRIENDS
Columbia University scientists place the time of the creation at 4,800,000,000 years ago, plus or minus 200,000,000 years.

The oldest-known village of the advanced Stone Age Indian people, who lived between 800 and 400 B.C., is discovered at Poverty Point, on Bayou Macon, Louisiana.

POVERTY POINT

INQUIRING MINDS WANT TO KNOW
According to a national survey conducted by the University of Illinois, children ask more questions about science than any other subject.

PASSING
Sir Alexander Fleming, 73 Nobel Prize winner in medicine for his discovery of penicillin, the Scottish-born Fleming was a captain in the Army Medical Corps during World War I and was knighted by the Queen of England.

Famous BIRTHS

Steve JOBS

Bill GATES

Nobel Prize Winners

PHYSICS
Polykarp Kusch, U.S.
Willis E. Lamb, U.S.
(work in atomic measurements)

CHEMISTRY
Vincent du Vigneaud, U.S.
(work with two hormones important in childbirth and control of blood pressure)

MEDICINE
A.H.T. Theorell, Sweden
(work on nature and function of oxidation enzymes)

1955

Victory OVER POLIO

A major medical hurdle is crossed as **Dr. Jonas Salk** discovers an anti-polio vaccine which will spread a mantle of protection over millions of American children. The discovery puts Dr. Salk into the rank of medical immortals.

Anxious parents line up to get their children inoculated.

POLIO SHOTS HERE ———▶

The effectiveness of the Salk vaccine is demonstrated in the greatest controlled experiment ever performed in medical history as the inoculation of 400,000 children proves successful in preventing poliomyelitis.

Matters *of the* Heart

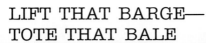

Several doctors report the use of transplants and plastic substitutes to restore normal blood flow to patients with hardened arteries.

An article written in the *Journal of the American Medical Association* says that carbonated soft drinks have become an X-ray aid as the carbonation forms a stomach bubble, making it easier to reveal heart defects.

The "Stethograph," developed by the Medical College of South Carolina, can pick up low-frequency vibrations of the heart which neither the human ear nor a stethoscope can hear.

BE STILL, MY BEATING HEART

A new X-ray device that will stop the heart's motion has been developed and promises to open the way to greater advances in the exciting new field of heart surgery.

LIFT THAT BARGE— TOTE THAT BALE

The United Press prints a report by a New York University doctor who asserts that people who take life easy are more likely to have heart trouble, diabetes and tooth decay than a hardworking day laborer.

Heart surgery is performed on all four valves.

A women's study conducted in Chicago on 13,000 deaths by heart disease reveals that professional women have a much lower death rate than housewives, one of the factors probably being diet.

The heart is found to have two zones, with severe disease of the inner one failing to show up on an electrocardiogram.

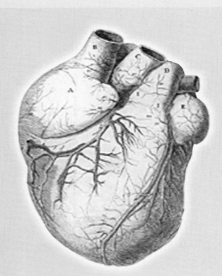

A report published in the YALE JOURNAL OF BIOLOGY AND MEDICINE states that experiments in the use of ultrasonic sound waves to dissolve kidney stones in cadavers has been successful and trials on humans could start in 1956 or 1957.

- - - -

Two British doctors report that body temperature can be quickly changed by placing a balloon in the stomach and then filling it with hot or cold water.

HOW SWEET IT IS!

Have a hangover? Have some honey! According to the *Journal of the American Women's Medical Association*, honey has been found to be one of the best treatments for acute intoxication, having both a sobering and sedative effect.

A new test for diagnosing tuberculosis has been developed by Dr. H.J. Corper, professor of medicine at the University of Colorado, which consists of injecting chemicals into a patient's arm. If the patient has the disease, there will be a reaction in about 30 seconds.

Doctors at the University of California report the first successful use of a steroid compound called Viadril as a surgical anesthetic.

IN THE MEANTIME, DRINK PLENTY OF LIQUIDS AND GET REST

A professor at the University of Michigan predicts that in the very foreseeable future a vaccine for the common cold will be developed.

General Electric develops a method of warming blood before it is transfused into babies affected with the Rh factor.

Use of radioactive substances to locate brain tumors reaches a higher rate of accuracy.

Scabies fades out as a disease.

Hand pain caused by gripping golf club handles too tightly can be relieved by wearing unfinished calf gloves, according to a Chicago doctor.

An article appearing in the journal *GP* states that about 80% of the U.S. population will suffer from chronic joint disorders by the time they are in their 50s or 60s.

THE WIGGLE FACTOR

An article appearing in *What's New* says that if you must sit for long periods of time, make sure you wiggle your toes and feet for circulation, thus helping to avoid a blood clot forming in a leg vein.

COLOR-BLIND STATS:
Men: 8%
Women: 1%

HENCEFORWARD KNOWN AS "THE KISSING DISEASE"

Kissing is reported responsible for infectious mononucleosis.

The chemical laboratory of the American Medical Association says that despite advertising claims to the contrary, decaffeinated coffee has some caffeine in it.

According to research done at the University of Michigan, some day it will be possible to isolate diseases that can be transmitted to offspring.

Prednisone developed as an alternative drug to cortisone.

New wonder drug, chlorpromazine, found to stop hiccups.

Vitamin B$_{12}$ discovered by Dorothy Hodgkin.

Frederick Sanger determines the molecular structure of insulin.

Spanish biochemist Severo Ochoa synthesizes RNA.

cancer

GOTTA TRY TO BEAT THOSE ODDS

The American Cancer Society reports that because of the aging population, cancer will strike one in every four Americans, which means that 40 million Americans will have cancer at some time in their lives.

NEW CANCER DETECTION TEST

Extensive research suggests that cancer of the cervix can be discovered early through routine microscopic examination of a smear.

A report made to the American College of Surgeons indicates that during surgery, under ultraviolet light, cancer cells will glow a bright red giving the surgeon a guide in determining the cancerous areas to be cut out.

TRUTH WINS OUT

A study of 1,000 people asking if they would like to be told the truth about having cancer reveals that an overwhelming majority said "yes."

Columbia Broadcasting System demonstrates a television microscope that can magnify minute objects such as cancer cells and corpuscles up to 15,000 times and project the image onto a 6-foot screen.

The Director of the U.S. Public Health Service's National Cancer Institute, Dr. John R. Heller, states on the Edward R. Murrow See It Now program that "the risk of acquiring lung cancer is greater among smokers than in nonsmokers."

THE SMOKING GUN

A study conducted by the American Cancer Society, which studied the smoking habits and health of 188,000 aging men, reveals some of the following:

- If you stop smoking now, you can still reduce the risk of lung cancer.
- The death rate among men who smoked two packs of cigarettes a day is about 90 times higher than that of nonsmokers.
- There is no significant association between cigar smoking and lung cancer.
- Pipe smoking appears to be associated with lung cancer but to a far lesser degree than cigarette smoking.
- Cancer of the larynx would be reduced by 80% if American men did not smoke.
- Heavy smoking, combined with heavy drinking, seems to add to the risk of cancer of the larynx.

Her Telephone...*prized possession in a lovely setting*

She's so proud of her lovely room, so very new and so nicely furnished to her particular tastes. It's her very own!

You just know that such a setting would not be complete without a telephone. Especially if it's in color!

It adds so much to the distinction of the room — and to the young lady who has been showing it off to her friends.

And it's so comforting and convenient to have the telephone close by!

BELL TELEPHONE SYSTEM

1955

THE BLESSINGS OF
AGING

- You won't procrastinate and will take action on matters that need to be taken care of.
- You'll be more emotional, such as crying more easily, more sensitive to criticism, impatient to wait and more high-strung.
- You will be less inclined to correct people.
- Your family relations will improve.
- You'll be friendlier to people.
- You'll depend more on other people for your happiness.
- Your interests will be more sedentary.
- You will read more about history, read the editorial page of your newspaper and lose interest in articles on crime.
- You will continue to be attracted to the opposite sex but less likely to talk about sex.
- You'll have more confidence and self-assurance.
- You'll find crowds and loud parties less appealing.
- You will be truthful and lay your cards on the table.

LIFE BEGINS AT 75

Once you bridge the difficult 60-75 age range, chances are good that you'll live to 100, according to a professor at New York Medical College.

KEEPING THOSE PEARLY WHITES PEARLY WHITE

Doctors at the Tufts College dental school find that chewing a stick of gum after eating sweet desserts clears decay-producing sugars from the mouth.

•

Preliminary results of a test conducted by Indiana University dentists show the incidence of decay in children's teeth nearly halved as a result of using an experimental toothpaste containing fluoride.

•

Dentures that blend with the natural colors of the mouth have been developed by Dr. Paul Chung, Northwest University Dental School.

According to a clinical professor of medicine at Philadelphia's Jefferson Medical College, obesity is a national tragedy and much more of a problem than polio.

PUT AWAY THOSE CHOCOLATE CHIP COOKIES, MOM

The fight against obesity must begin in childhood by instilling good eating habits, according to a Washington, D.C. physician.

HOW ABOUT SHOOTING A COUPLE OF BASKETS?

There are too many armchair athletes and not enough participation, says a psychiatrist at the University of California at Los Angeles.

WHAT A YEAR IT WAS!

SOME KIDS SWALLOW MANY AND DON'T WAKE UP IN THE MORNING

The American Medical Association is recommending as a safety feature that the warning "Keep Out of the Reach of Children" should appear on all bottles of aspirin.

EVERYBODY CALM DOWN!!!!

A tense home environment could produce peptic ulcers in infants and children, according to an article in *GP* magazine. Treatment is similar to that of adults.

DISPELLING SOME PREGNANCY MYTHS

- A baby will not be "marked" if the mother has a frightening experience during pregnancy.
- A mother does not lose a tooth for every pregnancy.
- The mother doesn't have to eat enough for two.
- There is no way to tell the sex of an infant until birth.
- Most babies are not born at night.
- Breast-feeding does not cause a larger appetite, breasts or waistline.
- Drinking coffee will not give your baby beauty marks.

1955 ADVERTISEMENT

NEW!

JOHNSON'S BABY SHAMPOO

WON'T BURN OR IRRITATE THE EYES

"No more tears from soap in the eyes"

GETS HAIR GLORIOUSLY CLEAN

Johnson's BABY SHAMPOO

59¢

The New York State Health Department issues a report to hospitals that the high incidence of blindness in premature babies is the result of administering oxygen following birth, a procedure in use since 1940.

NEED TO BE DRINKING MORE MOO JUICE

A study of over 400 pregnant women reveals a greater percentage of premature births occurring among those with poor nutrition, especially in women lacking enough calcium.

The *Yale Journal of Biology and Medicine* reports that a new improved pregnancy test has been perfected which yields results in only four hours or less, down from the present 48 to 96 hours.

MAKING AN APPOINTMENT WITH THE STORK

At a meeting of the American Congress of Obstetrics and Gynecology, a Philadelphia doctor suggests using the technique of elective labor induction, thereby allowing the mother-to-be and her doctor to choose a convenient time to have her baby.

Research done at Columbia University Teachers College demonstrates that if expectant mothers want their babies to be smart children, they should take plenty of vitamins during pregnancy and while nursing.

TWO HEADS ARE NOT BETTER THAN ONE

21-month-old Siamese twins flown in from Thailand are successfully separated at the University of Chicago Medical Center.

CLOSE YOUR EYES AND DON'T LOOK, MOM

Gentle roughhousing with Dad is an important part of your baby's development, says Dr. Ernest H. Watson of the University of Michigan.

WHAT! NO SCRUBBING UP BEFORE DINNER?

According to child-rearing guru Dr. Benjamin Spock, eating with dirty hands has never killed a child, so he suggests parents relax and not worry about it so much.

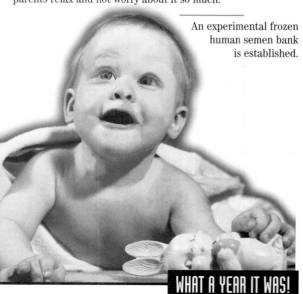

An experimental frozen human semen bank is established.

WHAT A YEAR IT WAS!

BE KIND TO YOUR BALD-HEADED FRIENDS

Wear your baldness proudly, as according to two Chicago doctors loss of hair is caused by the diminishment of fat in the scalp. Since they believe all humans will be bald someday, that puts you on a higher evolutionary rung than your hairy-headed friends.

MENTAL HEALTH

Tranquilizing substances such as thorazine and reserpine appear and revolutionize how the mentally disturbed are treated. While a decrease is seen in the use of electric shock therapy, Miltown gains popularity to reduce anxiety, induce sleep and as a muscle relaxant.

IF AT ONCE THEY DON'T SUCCEED...

Los Angeles Veterans Administration psychologists report that of the 20,000 or more suicides in the United States each year, almost three-quarters follow previous suicide attempts.

British medical journal *The Lancet* says that giving mental patients as much freedom as possible is very helpful in promoting their cure.

HE'S SCRATCHING HIS HEAD— I WONDER WHAT THAT MEANS
(Maybe His Head Is Just Itchy)

A new science called kinesics is the study of gestures as a key into the unconscious meaning of your every movement.

HANDCUFFS AND A FIFTH OF SCOTCH

According to an article in the *Journal of Criminal Law, Criminology and Police Science*, so-called "truth serum" is no more reliable for getting the truth out of people than a large shot of whiskey.

MAKING IT ON THEIR OWN

Young women who marry later tend to be better adjusted to life than those young women who rush into marriage.

Dr. Frederick Lemere of Seattle says that it is impossible for the alcoholic to drink moderately because of "factor X," which results from permanent destruction of the brain cells affecting the part of the brain that tells him to quit.

GOOD NEWS FOR WRIGLEY'S

The *Chicago Daily News* reports that workers who chew gum tend to be more efficient than their non-chewing gum counterparts as the gum helps to relieve tension.

LOOK INTO MY EYES... LOOK INTO MY EYES...

A University of Minnesota psychologist says that contrary to popular opinion, smart people are easier to hypnotize than people of lower intelligence.

Hypnosis for treatment of severe burn victims is being used in Dallas hospital.

Because America has an open class system, "social climbing" is popular but can cause ulcers because of the anxiety surrounding this "activity."

It's the neatest trick in home decorating! Exciting **GOLD SEAL**

wall-to-wall smooth

Just think what seamless wall-to-wall smooth surface flooring could do for you. It can give a sweep and beauty to your rooms not possible any other way for such a small amount of money. So easy to install, too! Just roll it out and trim to fit with a pair of scissors. It ends your floor cleaning problems—all you need is a damp mop. Here, surely, is the biggest change . . . for the least money . . . in the shortest space of time. And remember—Gold Seal "Congoleum," America's best-known enamel-surface floor covering, is still America's best buy.

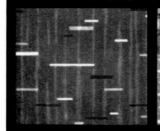

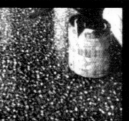

"Jackstraw" (Red— # 811) Also in 2 other colors. 6' x 9' to 12' x 15' rugs. Wall-to-wall—6', 9' or 12' wide.

"Plain and Fancy" (Green— # 481) Also in 4 other colors. 6' x 9' to 12' x 15' rugs.

"Cascade" (Rose— # 465) Also in 3 other colors. 6' x 9' to 12' x 15' rugs. Wall-to-wall —6', 9' or 12' wide.

"Sequin" (Charcoal— # 942) Also in 6 other colors. Wall-to-wall - 6', 9' or 12' wide.

"Heritage" (Beige— # 474) Also in 3 other colors. 6' x 9' to 12' x 15' rugs. Wall-to-wall—6', 9' or 12' wide.

surface flooring

ONLY GOLD SEAL CONGOLEUM* —wall-to-wall or in room-size rugs—gives you all this:

Most modern patterns ever offered, as well as lovely classical designs.

Lies flat without fastening. Just roll it out for a new floor in minutes. The only tool you need is a pair of scissors.

G-10 exclusive wonder formula, gives new gloss and super-smoothness to "Congoleum." A damp mop gets it sparkling clean.

You can move it from room to room or take it with you when you move.

Wears for years. Tests show "Congoleum" wears up to 1/3 longer than other enamel-surface floor coverings. The bright, clear colors of Gold Seal "Congoleum" are fade-resistant.

A Gold Seal guarantee of satisfaction or your money back—another Gold Seal exclusive that assures you of the highest quality.

Your Gold Seal dealer is now featuring Gold Seal "Congoleum"—wall-to-wall and room-sized rugs. See him soon. He's listed under "Linoleum" or "Floors" in the classified phone book.

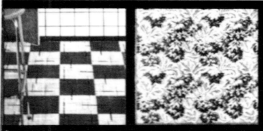

"Square-Tex" (Red — #945) Also in 3 other colors. Wall-to-wall —6', 9' or 12' wide.

"Spring Garden" (Grey — #415) Also in 3 other colors. 6' x 9' to 12' x 15' rugs.

139

1955 BUSINESS

Chase National Bank and the **Bank of Manhattan** agree to merge and form the second largest U.S. bank—the **Chase Manhattan Bank**.

Credit ratings are now accessible within one minute for over 300,000 merchants in New York's garment industry.

THE FIRST ORDER FOR JET-PROPELLED COMMERCIAL AIRCRAFT (20 BOEING 707 STRATOLINERS AND 25 DOUGLAS DC-8S) IS PLACED BY PAN AMERICAN WORLD AIRWAYS.

TRANS WORLD AIRLINES awards **LOCKHEED AIRCRAFT** record-breaking $70 million order for 24 high-speed airplanes.

AMERICAN MOTORS forms historic policy and issues first dealer 30-day used car guarantee.

PEPSI-COLA scores first bottle sales victory, knocking Coca-Cola out of first place in Chicago.

the flowers that bloom in the spring

Flowers are now purchased in European supermarkets, and Germany installs automats for selling flowers.

Improved methods of weed control through new pesticides are introduced.

The California flower industry suffers heavy losses in the fall as temperatures remain at 100 degrees for seven days.

Plastic flower pots rapidly replace clay pots throughout Europe.

The Netherlands outsells all other countries in the per capita purchase of flowers.

WHAT A YEAR IT WAS!

AFL-CIO MERGER

1,200 union delegates gather in New York for the most historic meeting in American labor.

The merger is destined to unite 16 million workers under one banner, a milestone for labor.

Symbolic of the AFL-CIO merger, George Meany and Walter Reuther jointly bang the gavel to open the meeting.

Meany becomes president of the newly formed organization with Reuther designated one of the 37 vice presidents.

GEORGE MEANY

was born and educated in New York City. He began his career as a plumbing apprentice in 1910 and began his labor career as a business representative of a plumbers local union in New York City, culminating in his election as president of the combined organization. Meany was recipient of the 1955 Laetare Medal of Notre Dame University as outstanding U.S. Roman Catholic layman.

UNEMPLOYMENT RANGES FROM A HIGH OF 5.3% TO A LOW OF 3.2%.

MEMBERSHIP IN THE AFL-CIO NUMBERS 15 MILLION.

YEARLY SALARIES

"I Love Lucy" 1954-1955 season, Lucille Ball & Desi Arnaz	$4 million
Industrial Engineer	$9,500
Auto Mechanic	$5,200
Foreman	$4,350
Salesman	$4,315
Radio Repairman	$3,960
Accountant	$3,640
Bartender	$3,380
Cocktail Waitress	$3,380
Stenographer	$3,120
Nurse	$3,000
Switchboard Operator	$2,400
Housekeeper	$1,300
Farm Laborer	$ 971

With the negotiating skills of United Mine Workers of America's President **John L. Lewis**, miners win a $20 daily salary, bringing their pay to the same amount as that of auto and steel workers.

THE AVERAGE WORKWEEK FOR WORKERS IN THE MANUFACTURING INDUSTRY IS 40.5 HOURS.

COPPER WORKERS STRIKE FOR 43 DAYS, EARNING A 15 1/2 CENTS AN HOUR RAISE.

Chairman of the Commission on Chronic Illness Leonard W. Mayo urges that the retirement age be advanced to 70 so that productive years can be expanded.

"take home blues"

MEDIAN FAMILY INCOME	**$4,421**
MEDIAN INCOME FOR MEN	**$3,400**
MEDIAN INCOME FOR WOMEN	**$1,100**

Don't Leave In A Huff

According to Dr. Alan Gregg of the Rockefeller Foundation, before quitting a job, relax for a week. *"Too many of the final decisions about changing one's job are made when one is too busy with other things,"* says Dr. Gregg.

WHAT A YEAR IT WAS!

Wheel Biz

The millionth **Volkswagen Beetle** rolls off the assembly line, resplendent with gold paint and rhinestones.

In January and February, consumers buy a record one million cars.

General Motors' Motorama car show features the **Oldsmobile Delta** and the **Pontiac Strato-Star**.

The Ford *Thunderbird* beats out Chevrolet's Corvette as the nation's favorite sports car.

Socony-Vacuum Oil Co. becomes Socony Mobil Oil Co., Inc.

Yamaha Motor Co., Ltd. is formed and begins selling one motorcycle model.

U.S. car manufacturers make approximately 170,000 cars a week, the highest number in the history of the industry.

WHAT A YEAR IT WAS!

STOCK EXCHANGE 1955

DOW JONES INDUSTRIAL AVERAGE:
High 488.40 (December)
Low 388.20 (January)
Avg. 442.72

TOTAL SHARES TRADED ON THE NEW YORK STOCK EXCHANGE — 650,000,000.

SEPTEMBER 26: STOCK EXCHANGE SUFFERS HEAVIEST ONE-DAY LOSS IN HISTORY—$14 BILLION—ATTRIBUTED TO IKE'S HEART ATTACK.

FORD MOTOR COMMON STOCK TO BE OFFERED TO THE PUBLIC FOR THE FIRST TIME NEXT YEAR.

GM GENERAL MOTORS COMMON STOCK IS SPLIT FOR THE FIRST TIME. IT IS THOUGHT TO BE THE LARGEST SINGLE COMMON STOCK OFFERING ANYWHERE.

A SEAT ON THE NEW YORK STOCK EXCHANGE SELLS FOR $70,000.

TRADING ON NEW YORK STOCK EXCHANGE REACHES HIGHEST VOLUME SINCE 1939.

STOCKS

Stock	Price
American Airlines	23 1/4
AT&T	179 1/4
CBS	23 1/2
Deere & Company	34 3/4
General Motors	138 3/4
Hilton Hotels	48 1/2
IBM	424
Montgomery Ward	81
Motorola	53
Pepsi-Cola	20 3/4
Pitney Bowes	49 1/2
Pittsburgh Steel	25 1/2
Safeway Stores	46
Shell Oil	60
Warner Bros.	20

SECRETARY AND BOSS AGREE...

The IBM Executive® Electric types America's most distinguished letters!

TO THE MEN WHO SIGN THE LETTERS:

Only IBM makes the EXECUTIVE Electric and only the EXECUTIVE is designed to make your letters look like the printing in a fine book. These letters make striking first impressions -- build company prestige. Don't you think your business would benefit if all your company correspondence were typed on IBM EXECUTIVE Electrics?

TO THE GIRLS WHO TYPE THE LETTERS:

Every secretary who types on an IBM Electric says she just couldn't go back to any other typewriter. That's because the lightest touch produces beautiful even typing on the IBM -- with less time, with less effort. Once you set finger to the IBM Electric you'll agree that it does more for you than any other typewriter.

THIS STANDARD AND THE "EXECUTIVE" shown in green are just 2 of the 32 IBM Electric models. They all come in many varying type faces and 7 handsome colors. When you replace your outdated manual, consider the IBM Electric. It gives you more for your money—yet it costs no more than other electrics. Call your nearest IBM office for more information.

 ELECTRIC TYPEWRITERS ...OUTSELL ALL OTHER ELECTRICS COMBINED!

Copr. International Business Machines Corp.

144

AMERICAN SHOE PRODUCTION REACHES A NEW RECORD HIGH: OVER 576 MILLION PAIRS.

THE FIRST COMPUTER FOR BUSINESS IS BROUGHT OUT BY **IBM**.

H&R Block
OPENS FOR BUSINESS.

Campbell's Soup Company takes over Swanson & Sons.

Lord & Taylor
OPENS A STORE IN PHILADELPHIA.

Samuel I. Newhouse purchases the St. Louis GLOBE-DEMOCRAT and radio station KWK for $6,250,000.

This Land Is My Land...
Henry J. Kaiser becomes the largest landowner on Waikiki, as he buys 16 1/2 acres for nearly $500,000. He plans to build a huge hotel complex.

MARION DAVIES buys the Desert Inn in Palm Springs for $2 million. She plans to create a miniature Rockefeller Center.

PASSINGS

Oscar Mayer, 95
Luncheon meat king, whose products remain lunchbox favorites.

Mario Peruzzi Sr., 80
President and cofounder of Planter's Nut and Chocolate Company.

Frank A. Seiberling, 95
Founder of Goodyear Tire and Rubber Company, Seiberling was a benevolent employer who cared about the safety and well-being of his workers. He invented many items, including a machine that makes tires.

Daniel J. Tobin, 80
Tobin was head of the International Brotherhood of Teamsters, Chauffeurs, Warehousemen and Helpers, the strongest division of the AFL, for 45 years.

President Eisenhower orders a 50% duty increase on imported bicycles.

AND NOW, A WORD FROM OUR GOVERNMENT

- The minimum wage increases to $1.00 per hour.
- The nation's third quarter **GROSS NATIONAL PRODUCT** is the highest in history—$392 billion. That equals goods and services in the ballpark of $2,376 for every American.
- The Department of Labor reports hourly wages of $1.90 per hour as of September.

WHAT A YEAR IT WAS!

This Is THE PRICE THAT WAS

FOOD BASKET

Angel Food Cake	$ .45
Apples (lb.)	.05
Avocados (each)	.10
Bananas (lb.)	.15
Bell Peppers (lb.)	.10
Blueberries (pt.)	.25
Box of Chocolates	2.50
Bread (loaf)	.17
Butter (lb.)	.59
Cake Mix	.25
Carrots (lb.)	.05
Cauliflower (each)	.10
Celery (lb.)	.02
Cheddar Cheese (lb.)	.59
Coffee (lb.)	.75
Corn (each)	.05
Cottage Cheese (pt.)	.25

(continued) FOOD BASKET

Crackers	$ .21	Orange Juice	$ .30
Cucumbers (ea.)	.05	Oranges (lb.)	.06
Date Bar Cookies	.23	Pancake Mix	.29
Eggs (dz.)	.47	Peanut Butter	.43
Grapes (lb.)	.07	Pears (lb.)	.08
Hershey Bar	.05	Pineapple (lb.)	.09
Ice Cream (1/2 gal.)	.89	Radishes (bunch)	.01
Jam	.35	Salad Dressing	.39
Ketchup	.19	Strawberries (bskt.)	.27
Lemons (lb.)	.09		
Lettuce (head)	.19	Swiss Cheese (lb.)	.57
Malted Milk Balls	.49	Syrup	.27
Mayonnaise	.49	Tomato Sauce	.05
Milk (qt.)	.20	Tuna	.25
Olive Oil	.51	Yams (lb.)	.09

ODDS & ENDS

"Santa Monica Outlook" Newspaper	$ .05
Bicycle	37.88
Broadway Musical, orchestra seat	7.50
Corvette	2,995.00
Davy Crockett Dancing Doll	5.96
Dr. Denton Footed Pajamas	2.75
Football	1.98
Gasoline (gal.)	.23
LP Record	1.99
Monopoly Game	2.49
Roller Skates	3.39
Stamp	.03
Tennis Balls	1.89
Tires	17.95

HOME SWEET HOME

U.S. AVERAGE:	$22,000

3-Bedroom House

Stamford, CT	$47,500
Miami Beach, FL	$41,000
Packanack Lake, NJ	$38,000
Scarsdale, NY	$35,000
Tenafly, NJ	$34,000
White Stone, VA	$30,000
Pacific Palisades, CA	$23,750
Cape Cod, MA	$22,500
Santa Monica, CA	$19,500
Woodland Hills, CA	$13,250
Queens, NY	$13,000

WHAT A YEAR IT WAS!

THIS OLD HOUSE

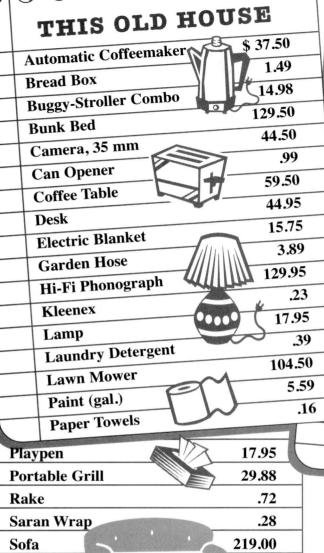

Automatic Coffeemaker	$ 37.50
Bread Box	1.49
Buggy-Stroller Combo	14.98
Bunk Bed	129.50
Camera, 35 mm	44.50
Can Opener	.99
Coffee Table	59.50
Desk	44.95
Electric Blanket	15.75
Garden Hose	3.89
Hi-Fi Phonograph	129.95
Kleenex	.23
Lamp	17.95
Laundry Detergent	.39
Lawn Mower	104.50
Paint (gal.)	5.59
Paper Towels	.16
Playpen	17.95
Portable Grill	29.88
Rake	.72
Saran Wrap	.28
Sofa	219.00
Toaster	27.50
Toilet Paper	.11
Toothpaste	.59
TV (21")	179.95

LA BOUTIQUE

FOR HER

Bra	$ 3.95
Dress	24.95
Girdle	4.95
Gloves	8.41
Hat	6.95
High Heel Shoes	26.95
Lipstick	.49
Nylons	1.00
Pajamas	3.95
Permanent	6.50
Purse	5.98
Rhinestone Jewelry	7.50
Suit	49.95
Trench Coat	29.95

(continued) LA BOUTIQUE

FOR HIM

Boxer Shorts	$ 1.25
Electric Shaver	29.50
Pajamas	4.95
Robe	12.95
Shoes	14.95
Silk Necktie	2.50
Slacks	10.95
Sports Coat	35.00
Sports Shirt	8.95
Suit	65.00

TRAVEL

Airfare: New York to Los Angeles	$ 80.00
Train: LA to SF (o/w)	6.50
Madrid to Barcelona (o/w)	9.50

MORTGAGES

THE FEDERAL HOUSING ADMINISTRATION
SHORTENS MORTGAGES TO 25 YEARS, THOUGH A HIGHER DOWN PAYMENT IS REQUIRED.

WHAT A YEAR IT WAS!

"But dear, you don't have to starve while dieting!"

said Elsie the Borden Cow

Elmer: You don't catch ME starving. I'll eat at the diner.

Elsie: Nobody's going to starve you, dear. I want to get you back in shape *without* starving you.

Elmer: AND WHAT'S WRONG WITH MY SHAPE?

Elsie: Nothing *much*—but you *can* pare it down and still eat plenty with Borden's Skimmed Milk as the basis of a low-calorie diet. Here, try it!

Elmer: Not half bad. Fill 'er up again and I'll stay home.

Elsie: Certainly, Elmer. It does my heart good to watch you drink it. You see, Borden's Skimmed Milk gives you the milk nourishment you need to keep up your pep while dieting. But it has only *half* the calories of whole milk!

Elmer: Skip the sales talk, Elsie, and fill up that glass.

Vital part of your diet...
Borden's Fresh Skimmed Milk
gives real milk nourishment
without the fat!

ALL ABOARD! ALL A-BORDEN'S

Get Borden's Skimmed Milk on Elsie's Good Food Line!
At your food store, or at your door!

DISASTERS

HURRICANE CAROL

400 perish as densely populated northeastern states are dealt two staggering blows back to back: Hurricane Carol and a 9-inch deluge combine to reduce some of the nation's oldest cities to shambles. Property loss reaches hundreds of millions of dollars.

Whiting, Indiana

is almost engulfed in flames and smoke that rise 400 feet into the air as an oil refinery fire burns out of control for more than two days on the shores of Lake Michigan.

Upwards of four million gallons of high-octane gasoline pose an almost impossible task for firefighters summoned from every surrounding community.

In addition to the towering flames, a series of blasts rock the entire countryside.

Despite the heroic efforts by firefighters, the explosions hurl tons of sheet metal from storage tanks into the community, causing two deaths and devastating property losses.

The force of the blast can be seen from the caved-in walls and upended cars tossed several hundred feet.

By the time the holocaust has been brought under control, damage estimates reach $10 million—one of the worst fires of its kind on record.

WHAT A YEAR IT WAS!

THE WORST DISASTER SINCE THE SAN FRANCISCO EARTHQUAKE HITS NORTHERN CALIFORNIA

Flooding caused by torrential rains results in property damage estimated at $150 million.

THE FORCE OF THE FLOOD'S ATTACK RIPS HOMES FROM THEIR FOUNDATIONS AND FLOATS THEM AWAY LIKE TOY BOATS.

Makeshift refugee centers are set up to house some of the 50,000 people left homeless by this devastating flood.

WHAT A YEAR IT WAS!

1955

NATION'S WORST AIR DISASTERS

Two tragedies with a common destination—Denver, Colorado—end disastrously in the Rocky Mountains. First, a deliberate act of sabotage, a time bomb, takes the lives of 44 people.

The second crash, near Laramie, Wyoming, results in 66 fatalities and is reported to be the worst commercial aviation accident in U.S. history.

Christmas week automobile fatalities reach a record high.

disasters around the world — 1955

february:

165 injured and 14 killed when a spectator grandstand at a bullring stadium in Hunucma, Mexico collapses.

18 people lose their lives and 180 are missing when a blizzard strikes Japan.

april:

The Philippines are devastated by severe earthquakes, resulting in 432 deaths and more than 2,000 injuries.

13 Holy Week travelers are killed and 90 hurt when their railroad cars derail, plummeting into a canyon near Alsaba, Mexico.

may:

154 reported dead when a ferryboat and freighter collide in the Sea of Japan.

Tornadoes kill 125 and injure 700, leaving a wake of destruction in Kansas, Missouri, Oklahoma and Texas.

june:

500 reported dead as a tidal wave hits near Patani, Thailand.

july:

Severe summer heat wave in Great Britain and Western Europe causes the death of 429 people.

august:

Soviet airliner crashes near Voronezh in the U.S.S.R., killing all 25 passengers, including 10 women members of the Norwegian parliament.

september:

$15 million property damage and six deaths result from a week of raging forest fires in the Santa Barbara, California area.

BASEBALL SPORTS 1955

Brooklyn Dodgers, with Johnny Podres pitching, beat New York Yankees 4-3, winning their first World Series.

CIRCULATION 3

DAILY

BASEBALL HALL OF FAME INDUCTS SIX PLAYERS

Six baseball greats join the ranks of baseball giants by winning election into the Hall of Fame. The group includes **Home Run Baker, Joe DiMaggio, Gabby Hartnett, Ted Lyons, Ray Schalk** and **Dazzy Vance**.

Joe DiMaggio

Racking up 175 home runs, the New York Yankees are the American League home run champs, with switch-hitter **Mickey Mantle** delivering 37 of them.

Mickey Mantle becomes the first New York Yankee to hit a home run to straightaway center at Yankee Stadium. The epic blast travels well over the 30-foot hitter's backdrop and lands in the ninth row of the bleachers for an estimated total of 486 feet.

Mickey Mantle

1955 BASEBALL ● NEWS

Leo Durocher, manager of the New York Giants since 1948, resigns to enter private business.

Chicago newspaperman **Arch Ward**, originator of the All-Star Game, dies suddenly at the age of 58 on his way to cover the 22nd Midsummer Classic.

- Kansas City is the new home of the Philadelphia Athletics.

- **Roberto Clemente** plays right field for the first time for the Pittsburgh Pirates.

- The Brooklyn Dodgers beat the Pittsburgh Pirates 6-2 in a game where pitcher **Don Newcombe** becomes the only National League pitcher of the decade to steal home in the ninth inning. Newcombe also sets another National League record with seven home runs, the most ever by a pitcher.

- **Joe DiMaggio's** 13-year-old son, **Joe Jr.**, gets a Most Valuable Player award at Black-Foxe Military School in Los Angeles.

- **Stan Musial** hits a homer in the 12th inning to win the All-Star Game for the National League.

- Chicago Cubs shortstop **Ernie Banks** hits his fifth grand-slam home run of the season, setting a major league record.

New York Giant **Willie Mays** joins fellow sluggers **Babe Ruth, Ralph Kiner, Jimmie Foxx, Hank Greenberg, Hack Wilson** and **Johnny Mize** as a member of baseball's prestigious "50 Club," becoming only the seventh player ever to hit 50 home runs in a single season.

Willie Mays

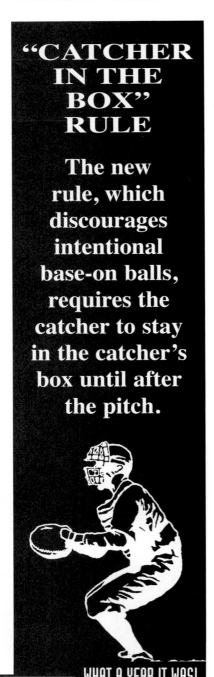

"CATCHER IN THE BOX" RULE

The new rule, which discourages intentional base-on balls, requires the catcher to stay in the catcher's box until after the pitch.

WHAT A YEAR IT WAS!

BASEBALL'S ★★★ ALL-STAR TEAM

AMERICAN LEAGUE

YOGI BERRA (New York)
JIM FINIGAN (Kansas City)
NELLIE FOX (Chicago)
AL KALINE (Detroit)
HARVEY KUENN (Detroit)
MICKEY MANTLE (New York)
MICKEY VERNON (Washington)
TED WILLIAMS (Boston)

NATIONAL LEAGUE

ERNIE BANKS (Chicago)
ROY CAMPANELLA (Brooklyn)
DEL ENNIS (Philadelphia)
TED KLUSZEWSKI (Cincinnati)
EDDIE MATHEWS (Milwaukee)
DON MUELLER (New York)
RED SCHOENDIENST (St. Louis)
DUKE SNIDER (Brooklyn)

Home Run Leaders
National League
Willie Mays (New York, 51)
American League
Mickey Mantle (New York, 37)

Batting Champions
National League
Richie Ashburn (Philadelphia, .338)
American League
Al Kaline (Detroit, .340)

Most Valuable Player
National League
Roy Campanella (Brooklyn)
American League
Yogi Berra (New York)

Strikeouts
National League
Sam Jones (Chicago, 198)
American League
Herb Score (Cleveland, 245)

Rookie Of The Year
National League
Bill Virdon (St. Louis)
American League
Herb Score (Cleveland)

The All-Star Game
National League
over
American League
6-5

Elston Howard

Elston Howard becomes the first black to play for the New York Yankees.

New York Yankees catcher Elston Howard announces that he stays at all hotels white members of the team use except in Baltimore.

Chicago Cub **Sam Jones** becomes the first black pitcher to throw a major league no-hitter.

WHAT A YEAR IT WAS!

1955

1955

FOOTBALL

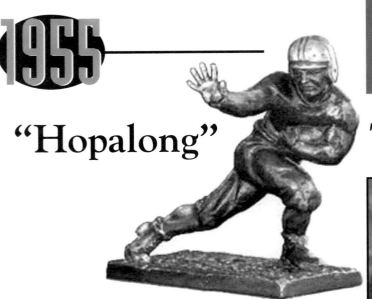

"Hopalong" Takes Heisman

Raymond Tierney, president of New York's Downtown Athletic Club, presents the highly coveted Heisman Memorial Trophy to **Howard "Hopalong" Cassady** of Ohio State, the top college star of the year.

A two-time all-American halfback, "Hopalong" wins the award after scoring the greatest majority of points in history. Sportswriters and sportscasters make him a landslide winner.

Drafted by the Detroit Lions, Cassady climaxes four sensational seasons at Ohio State by scoring 15 touchdowns.

Cassady's pretty wife seals the joyous occasion with a big kiss.

1955

88,000 fans pack the Los Angeles Coliseum to watch the **Cleveland Browns beat the Los Angeles Rams for the National Football League championship, 38-14.**

Ram **Norman Van Brocklin** *(above)* passes to **Skeets Quinlan** *(left)* for first score of the game.

Browns quarterback **Otto Graham Jr.** makes his farewell appearance closing out his grid career in brilliant style with another incredible pass *(right)*.

Graham, the National Football League's Most Valuable Player, ends his 10-year career with a completion average of 55.8%. The 38-14 victory is a fine farewell gift from Graham to Coach **Paul Brown**— his third NFL crown in six years.

WHAT A YEAR IT WAS!

TOP 5 COLLEGIATE FOOTBALL TEAMS

① **University of Oklahoma**

② **Michigan State**

③ **Maryland**

④ **University of California at Los Angeles**

⑤ **Ohio State**

NFL PRO BOWL
West over East, 26-19

NATIONAL COLLEGE FOOTBALL CHAMPIONS
Oklahoma, 11-0-0

ROSE BOWL
Ohio State over USC, 20-7

SOUTHEASTERN CONFERENCE CHAMPIONSHIP
Mississippi over Mississippi State, 26-0

NEW SUBSTITUTION RULE

A player is now permitted to reenter the game once during the same quarter in which he was removed from the lineup. Formerly, a player could not play in the same period except during the last four minutes of the second and fourth quarters.

Gov. Marvin Griffin petitions the Georgia Board of Regents to ban the Georgia Tech football team from the Sugar Bowl because its opponent, the University of Pittsburgh, has a black player on the team. The petition is turned down.

WHAT A YEAR IT WAS!

250 HP Chrysler New Yorker Deluxe St. Regis in Navajo Orange and Desert Sand

ANNOUNCING America's most smartly different car

CHRYSLER FOR 1955

WITH THE NEW 100-MILLION-DOLLAR LOOK

Everything about this dazzling Chrysler is completely new and dramatically different. It brings you a totally *new* fashion in modern motor car design.

The new Chrysler is inches lower in its sweeping silhouette . . . washed free of clutter . . . purposeful as an arrow shot from a bow. Its sleek new <u>100-Million-Dollar Look</u> will make you feel like a hundred million dollars the *instant* you step inside!

And in performance this magnificent new Chrysler stands above all others. *All*

Chryslers are now V-8 powered with engines up to 250 HP . . . with Power-Flite, the only *fully-automatic* no-clutch drive that works without jerking or "time lag" . . . with the added safety of Power Brakes and the feather-light control of Chrysler *Full-time* coaxial Power Steering.

No other car on the road can offer you such an exciting sense of personal *power* and personal *pride*. Visit your Chrysler dealer today and see why now, more than ever before, *the power of leadership is yours in a Chrysler.*

161

1955

Enthusiastic fans gather at New York's Madison Square Garden to watch the St. Louis Billikens take on St. John's Redmen.

BASKETBALL

One disappointed fan reacts as St. Louis steals the ball and scores a basket.

This fiercely competitive game has fans going crazy as the score keeps flip-flopping.

After a 14-point scoring spree during the last four minutes of play, St. Louis takes the win 88-80.

WHAT'S THE LATEST COLLEGE HOOPLA?

NCAA CHAMPIONS
San Francisco over
La Salle, 77-63

•

NCAA MOST OUTSTANDING PLAYER
Bill Russell
San Francisco

•

7'2"
Wilt Chamberlain
to attend the
University of Kansas.

Wilt Chamberlain

WHAT A YEAR IT WAS!

1955

ALL-STAR PROFESSIONALS

WEST	**EAST**
LARRY FOUST (Fort Wayne Pistons)	**BOB COUSY** (Boston Celtics)
VERN MIKKELSEN (Minneapolis Lakers)	**NEIL JOHNSTON** (Philadelphia Warriors)
BOB PETTIT (Milwaukee Hawks)	**DICK McGUIRE** (N.Y. Knickerbockers)
BOBBY WANZER (Rochester Royals)	**DOLPH SCHAYES** (Syracuse Nationals)
GEORGE YARDLEY (Fort Wayne Pistons)	**BILL SHARMAN** (Boston Celtics)

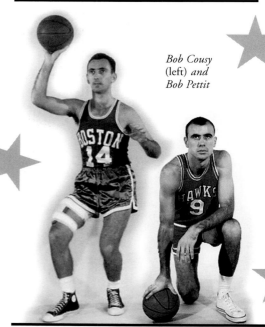

*Bob Cousy
(left) and
Bob Pettit*

The 1955 All-Star Game, played in New York, saw the Boston Celtics' **Bob Cousy** and **Bill Sharman** lead the East to a 100-91 victory over the West.

NBA CHAMPIONS

Syracuse Nationals
over
Fort Wayne Pistons
4-3

•

NBA SCORING LEADER

Neil Johnston
Philadelphia
22.7 average

•

NBA REBOUND LEADER

Neil Johnston
Philadelphia
15.1 average

•

NBA ASSISTS

Bob Cousy
Boston
557

•

NBA FREE THROW PERCENTAGE

Bill Sharman
Boston
.897

•

NBA ROOKIE OF THE YEAR

Bob Pettit
Milwaukee

WHAT A YEAR IT WAS!

BOXING

HEAVYWEIGHT
ROCKY MARCIANO

LIGHT HEAVYWEIGHT
ARCHIE MOORE

MIDDLEWEIGHT
CARL "BOBO" OLSON
SUGAR RAY ROBINSON

WELTERWEIGHT
TONY DEMARCO
CARMEN BASILIO

LIGHTWEIGHT
JAMES CARTER
WALLACE "BUD" SMITH

FEATHERWEIGHT
SANDY SADDLER

RING Magazine
FIGHTER OF
THE YEAR
ROCKY MARCIANO

Rocky Marciano, undefeated world heavyweight champion, defends his title twice, knocking out Great Britain's **Don Cockell** and later in the year, **Archie Moore**. Marciano fights a total of 49 unbeaten professional bouts.

The **BOXING HALL OF FAME**, housed in the Ring Museum in Madison Square Garden, votes in 10 new members:

Abe Attell • Harry Greb • Sam Langford
Benny Leonard • Terry McGovern
William Richmond • William Thompson
Gene Tunney • Joe Walcott
Mickey Walker

❖

They join the ranks of other boxing greats such as:
John L. Sullivan • Daniel Mendoza
Jack Dempsey • John C. Heenan
Bob Fitzsimmons • Jack Johnson
and *Joe Louis*

The heavyweight title bout held at New York's Yankee Stadium between **Rocky Marciano** and **Archie Moore** attracts 61,574 fans and is screened exclusively for television and theater viewing in 133 theaters and drive-ins in 92 cities for an additional 350,000 people.

Coming out of retirement, **Sugar Ray Robinson** knocks out **Carl "Bobo" Olson** in the second round, becoming the first fighter to return to the ring and win back a title as well as the first to capture the middleweight championship three times.

1955 GOLF NEWS

▼ **Jack Fleck** defeats four-time U.S. Open golf champion **Ben Hogan** in a surprise victory in an 18-hole play-off.

▼ **Professional Golfers Association** Championship goes to **Doug Ford**, who defeats **Cary Middlecoff** 4-3.

▼ Australia's **Peter Thomson** retains the British Open crown.

| **ARNOLD PALMER** wins the Canadian Open. |

The Ladies Have Their Day

Pat Lesser takes the U.S. Women's Amateur Championship, **Fay Crocker** wins the U.S. Women's Open Championship and **Beverly Hanson** beats **Louise Suggs** 4-3, winning the Women's Professional Golfers Association title.

The golf cart

gains increasing popularity and allows the physically impaired to hit the links again.

golf STATISTICS

U.S. OPEN	Jack Fleck Fay Crocker
PGA/LPGA	Doug Ford Beverly Hanson
PGA/LPGA LEADING MONEY WINNER	Julius Boros $63,122 Patty Berg $16,492
PGA PLAYER OF THE YEAR	Doug Ford
MASTERS	Cary Middlecoff
U.S. AMATEUR	Harvie Ward Patricia Lesser
BRITISH OPEN	Peter Thomson
SENIOR PGA	Mortie Dutra

WHAT A YEAR IT WAS!

HOCKEY

STANLEY CUP CHAMPIONS
Detroit Red Wings over **Montreal Canadiens**, 4-3

ROSS TROPHY (Leading Scorer)
Bernie "Boom Boom" Geoffrion, Montreal

LADY BING MEMORIAL TROPHY (Most Gentlemanly Player)
Sid Smith, Toronto

VEZINA TROPHY (Outstanding Goalie)
Terry Sawchuk, Detroit

HART MEMORIAL TROPHY (MVP)
Ted Kennedy, Toronto

CALDER MEMORIAL TROPHY (Rookie of the Year)
Ed Litzenberger, Chicago

Canada retains world hockey championship, beating U.S.S.R. 5-0.

100 people are arrested as hockey fans riot in Montreal to protest NHL president's suspension of Maurice "The Rocket" Richard.

Hoping for a place on the Olympic bobsled squad, members of the U.S. Air Force take some practice spins on the icy runs in the German Alps.

In bobsledding, close teamwork is essential from start to finish.

GROSSINGER'S NEW YORK
plays host to the 10th Annual Barrel Jumping Competition.

Leo Lebel leads off with the first jump. Lebel sets a new record of 28 feet 7 inches, winning the World Barrel Jumping Championship.

WHAT A YEAR IT WAS!

167

1955
HORSE RACING

KENTUCKY DERBY
Swaps ridden by
Willie Shoemaker

PREAKNESS STAKES
Nashua ridden by **Eddie Arcaro**

BELMONT STAKES
Nashua ridden by **Eddie Arcaro**

HORSE OF THE YEAR
Nashua

MONEY LEADERS
Jockey: **Eddie Arcaro** $1,864,796
Horse: *Nashua* $752,550

RACING NEWS

The new home of the National Museum of Racing, located in Saratoga Springs, New York, is dedicated by **Governor W. Averell Harriman**, at the site of the historic Saratoga Racetrack.

The **William Woodward Jr.** estate pays $1,251,200 for the champion racehorse *Nashua*.

Hanover Shoe Farms, of Hanover, Pennsylvania, pays a record $500,000 for *Adios*, a 15-year-old stallion, purchased from Meadowlands Farms.

BOWLING

THE PFEIFFER'S BEER FIVE of Detroit, Michigan win the American Bowling Congress Open team title for the third time.

BOWLER OF THE YEAR
STEVE NAGY
SYLVIA WENE

BPAA ALL-STAR TOURNAMENT
STEVE NAGY
SYLVIA WENE (Jan.)
ANITA CANTALINE (Dec.)

U.S. Match Game Bowling Champion
STEVE NAGY

TENNIS

U.S. OPEN

Tony Trabert over **Ken Rosewall**

Doris Hart over **Patricia Ward**

WIMBLEDON

Tony Trabert over **Kurt Nielsen**

Louise Brough over **Beverly Fleitz**

TALK AROUND THE NET

Retired from tennis, the world's greatest female tennis star, 21-year-old **Maureen "Little Mo" Connolly**, is the new women's sports editor for *The San Diego Union* and writes her first column in which she complains about the state of the American sports scene.

New York's WNBT does the first color broadcast of a Davis Cup match played at the West Side Tennis Club in Forest Hills.

Australia wins back Davis Cup from America 5-0 in Forest Hills match.

From left: (American Team) Tony Trabert, Vic Seixas; (Australian Team) Lewis Hoad, Rex Hartwig

1955 AUTO RACING

Bill Vukovich

Seeking a third consecutive win in the Indy 500, **Bill Vukovich** is killed in the 57th lap in a pileup while leading the field.

LE MANS
Mike Hawthorn & Ivor Bueb, Jaguar D, 107.05 mph

WINSTON CUP
Tim Flock

INDIANAPOLIS 500
Bob Sweikert, John Zink Special, 128.213 mph

At the Le Mans car race, French driver **Pierre Levegh** along with at least 80 spectators die in the worst accident in auto racing history. A temporary racing ban is ordered by the French Cabinet.

BILLIARDS

WORLD POCKET BILLIARD CHAMPIONSHIP

Irving Crane of Binghamton, New York wins a four-man round-robin tournament in Philadelphia taking the crown from **Willie Mosconi,** the world pocket-billiard champion since 1950.

Figure Skating

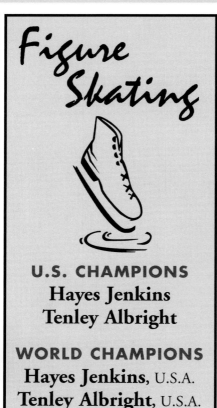

U.S. CHAMPIONS
Hayes Jenkins
Tenley Albright

WORLD CHAMPIONS
Hayes Jenkins, U.S.A.
Tenley Albright, U.S.A.

RODEO

ALL-AROUND CHAMPION COWBOY

Casey Tibbs

chess

WORLD CHAMPIONS
Mikhail Botvinnik (U.S.S.R.)
Elizaveta Bykova (U.S.S.R.)

U.S. CHAMPIONS
Arthur Bisguier
Gisela K. Gresser
Nancy Roos

CYCLING
TOUR de FRANCE
Louison Bobet
France
(wins for the third time)

DOG SHOW WINNER
WESTMINSTER KENNEL CLUB
KIPPAX FEARNOUGHT
Bulldog

BEST IN SHOW

SOFTBALL

MAJOR FAST PITCH
MEN   Raybestos Cardinals, Stratford, CT
WOMEN Orange County Lionettes, Orange, CA

TRACK & FIELD

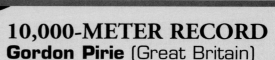

BOSTON MARATHON
Hideo Hamamura (Japan)

5,000-METER RECORD
Vladimir Kuts (Soviet Union)
13:46.8 Minutes

10,000-METER RECORD
Gordon Pirie (Great Britain)
29.19 Minutes

U.S. runner **Louis Jones** sets the 400-meter mark at 44.5 seconds.

2,000 athletes compete in the Pan American Games held in Mexico City.

OUTSTANDING FEMALE ATHLETES

BOWLING

SYLVIA WENE

Winner of the U.S. Match Game Bowling Championship women's crown

SOFTBALL PITCHING

MARGIE LAW

All-American for 6 of the last 7 years

DIVING

PAT KELLER McCORMICK

Winner of a record 18 national titles, Olympic & Pan American Games champion

SAILING

TONI MONETTI

Winner of the Mrs. Charles Francis Adams Cup

SKIING

JILL KINMONT

Sets record by winning both Women's National Junior & Senior Slalom

---

AP ATHLETE OF THE YEAR

Howard "Hopalong" Cassady
college football

Patty Berg
golf

•

SPORTS ILLUSTRATED SPORTSMAN OF THE YEAR

Johnny Podres
baseball

•

JAMES E. SULLIVAN MEMORIAL AWARD

Harrison Dillard
track

•

THE HICKOK BELT

Otto Graham
football

172

WHAT A YEAR IT WAS!

ONE IN FOUR

Competing in London, three men (Hungary's **Laszlo Tabori** and Great Britain's **Brian Hewson** and **Chris Chataway**) break records by running a mile in four minutes.

The Soviet Union announces it will participate in the 1956 Olympic games in Melbourne, Australia.

famous births

Otis **B**irdsong
Earl **C**ampbell
Olga **K**orbut
Moses **M**alone
Edwin **M**oses
Greg **N**orman
Robin **Y**ount

SPEEDBOAT RACING RECORD BROKEN

Donald Campbell, of England, breaks the 200 mph speedboat mark, setting a record of 216.2 mph in a race on Lake Mead, Nevada. His dad, **Sir Malcolm Campbell**, is the former record holder.

PASSINGS

CLARK GRIFFITH, 85
Player, manager and team owner, Baseball Hall of Famer Griffith was instrumental in organizing the American League.

HONUS WAGNER, 81
One of the first players inducted into the Baseball Hall of Fame and eight-time National League batting champ, Wagner was thought to be the best shortstop in history. He was the National League Batting Champion a record eight times, played in 2,785 games and scored close to 1,800 runs.

CY YOUNG, 88
One of baseball's greatest pitchers, he was the third pitcher to be voted into the Baseball Hall of Fame. His lightning pitch set new records, including most games pitched (906) and most games won (511).

1955 WAS A GREAT YEAR, BUT...

THE BEST IS YET TO COME!